C-3275   **CAREER EXAMINATION SERIES**   

OCEANSIDE LIBRARY
30 DAVISON AVENUE
OCEANSIDE, NEW YORK
PHONE (516) 766-2360

THIS IS YOUR **PASSBOOK**® FOR ...

REAL PROPERTY APPRAISER– ARBITRATOR

NATIONAL LEARNING CORPORATION®
passbooks.com

DEC 0 8 2020

COPYRIGHT NOTICE

This book is SOLELY intended for, is sold ONLY to, and its use is RESTRICTED to individual, bona fide applicants or candidates who qualify by virtue of having seriously filed applications for appropriate license, certificate, professional and/or promotional advancement, higher school matriculation, scholarship, or other legitimate requirements of educational and/or governmental authorities.

This book is NOT intended for use, class instruction, tutoring, training, duplication, copying, reprinting, excerption, or adaptation, etc., by:

1) Other publishers
2) Proprietors and/or Instructors of «Coaching» and/or Preparatory Courses
3) Personnel and/or Training Divisions of commercial, industrial, and governmental organizations
4) Schools, colleges, or universities and/or their departments and staffs, including teachers and other personnel
5) Testing Agencies or Bureaus
6) Study groups which seek by the purchase of a single volume to copy and/or duplicate and/or adapt this material for use by the group as a whole without having purchased individual volumes for each of the members of the group
7) Et al.

Such persons would be in violation of appropriate Federal and State statutes.

PROVISION OF LICENSING AGREEMENTS. — Recognized educational, commercial, industrial, and governmental institutions and organizations, and others legitimately engaged in educational pursuits, including training, testing, and measurement activities, may address request for a licensing agreement to the copyright owners, who will determine whether, and under what conditions, including fees and charges, the materials in this book may be used them. In other words, a licensing facility exists for the legitimate use of the material in this book on other than an individual basis. However, it is asseverated and affirmed here that the material in this book CANNOT be used without the receipt of the express permission of such a licensing agreement from the Publishers. Inquiries re licensing should be addressed to the company, attention rights and permissions department.

All rights reserved, including the right of reproduction in whole or in part, in any form or by any means, electronic or mechanical, including photocopying, recording, or by any information storage and retrieval system, without permission in writing from the Publisher.

Copyright © 2020 by

NLC®

National Learning Corporation

212 Michael Drive, Syosset, NY 11791
(516) 921-8888 • www.passbooks.com
E-mail: info@passbooks.com

PUBLISHED IN THE UNITED STATES OF AMERICA

PASSBOOK® SERIES

THE *PASSBOOK® SERIES* has been created to prepare applicants and candidates for the ultimate academic battlefield – the examination room.

At some time in our lives, each and every one of us may be required to take an examination – for validation, matriculation, admission, qualification, registration, certification, or licensure.

Based on the assumption that every applicant or candidate has met the basic formal educational standards, has taken the required number of courses, and read the necessary texts, the *PASSBOOK® SERIES* furnishes the one special preparation which may assure passing with confidence, instead of failing with insecurity. Examination questions – together with answers – are furnished as the basic vehicle for study so that the mysteries of the examination and its compounding difficulties may be eliminated or diminished by a sure method.

This book is meant to help you pass your examination provided that you qualify and are serious in your objective.

The entire field is reviewed through the huge store of content information which is succinctly presented through a provocative and challenging approach – the question-and-answer method.

A climate of success is established by furnishing the correct answers at the end of each test.

You soon learn to recognize types of questions, forms of questions, and patterns of questioning. You may even begin to anticipate expected outcomes.

You perceive that many questions are repeated or adapted so that you can gain acute insights, which may enable you to score many sure points.

You learn how to confront new questions, or types of questions, and to attack them confidently and work out the correct answers.

You note objectives and emphases, and recognize pitfalls and dangers, so that you may make positive educational adjustments.

Moreover, you are kept fully informed in relation to new concepts, methods, practices, and directions in the field.

You discover that you arre actually taking the examination all the time: you are preparing for the examination by "taking" an examination, not by reading extraneous and/or supererogatory textbooks.

In short, this PASSBOOK®, used directedly, should be an important factor in helping you to pass your test.

REAL PROPERTY APPRAISER-ARBITRATOR

DUTIES
Negotiates claim settlements on pending tax certiorari proceedings; performs related duties as required.

SUBJECT OF EXAMINATION
Written test designed to test for knowledge, skills, and/or abilities in such areas as:
1. Real property terminology, documents and forms;
2. Laws and judicial decisions applicable to the taxation of real property;
3. Principles, practices and theory of real property valuation and assessment; and
4. Preparing written material.

HOW TO TAKE A TEST

I. YOU MUST PASS AN EXAMINATION

A. *WHAT EVERY CANDIDATE SHOULD KNOW*
	Examination applicants often ask us for help in preparing for the written test. What can I study in advance? What kinds of questions will be asked? How will the test be given? How will the papers be graded?
	As an applicant for a civil service examination, you may be wondering about some of these things. Our purpose here is to suggest effective methods of advance study and to describe civil service examinations.
	Your chances for success on this examination can be increased if you know how to prepare. Those "pre-examination jitters" can be reduced if you know what to expect. You can even experience an adventure in good citizenship if you know why civil service exams are given.

B. *WHY ARE CIVIL SERVICE EXAMINATIONS GIVEN?*
	Civil service examinations are important to you in two ways. As a citizen, you want public jobs filled by employees who know how to do their work. As a job seeker, you want a fair chance to compete for that job on an equal footing with other candidates. The best-known means of accomplishing this two-fold goal is the competitive examination.
	Exams are widely publicized throughout the nation. They may be administered for jobs in federal, state, city, municipal, town or village governments or agencies.
	Any citizen may apply, with some limitations, such as the age or residence of applicants. Your experience and education may be reviewed to see whether you meet the requirements for the particular examination. When these requirements exist, they are reasonable and applied consistently to all applicants. Thus, a competitive examination may cause you some uneasiness now, but it is your privilege and safeguard.

C. *HOW ARE CIVIL SERVICE EXAMS DEVELOPED?*
	Examinations are carefully written by trained technicians who are specialists in the field known as "psychological measurement," in consultation with recognized authorities in the field of work that the test will cover. These experts recommend the subject matter areas or skills to be tested; only those knowledges or skills important to your success on the job are included. The most reliable books and source materials available are used as references. Together, the experts and technicians judge the difficulty level of the questions.
	Test technicians know how to phrase questions so that the problem is clearly stated. Their ethics do not permit "trick" or "catch" questions. Questions may have been tried out on sample groups, or subjected to statistical analysis, to determine their usefulness.
	Written tests are often used in combination with performance tests, ratings of training and experience, and oral interviews. All of these measures combine to form the best-known means of finding the right person for the right job.

II. HOW TO PASS THE WRITTEN TEST

A. NATURE OF THE EXAMINATION

To prepare intelligently for civil service examinations, you should know how they differ from school examinations you have taken. In school you were assigned certain definite pages to read or subjects to cover. The examination questions were quite detailed and usually emphasized memory. Civil service exams, on the other hand, try to discover your present ability to perform the duties of a position, plus your potentiality to learn these duties. In other words, a civil service exam attempts to predict how successful you will be. Questions cover such a broad area that they cannot be as minute and detailed as school exam questions.

In the public service similar kinds of work, or positions, are grouped together in one "class." This process is known as *position-classification*. All the positions in a class are paid according to the salary range for that class. One class title covers all of these positions, and they are all tested by the same examination.

B. FOUR BASIC STEPS

1) Study the announcement

How, then, can you know what subjects to study? Our best answer is: "Learn as much as possible about the class of positions for which you've applied." The exam will test the knowledge, skills and abilities needed to do the work.

Your most valuable source of information about the position you want is the official exam announcement. This announcement lists the training and experience qualifications. Check these standards and apply only if you come reasonably close to meeting them.

The brief description of the position in the examination announcement offers some clues to the subjects which will be tested. Think about the job itself. Review the duties in your mind. Can you perform them, or are there some in which you are rusty? Fill in the blank spots in your preparation.

Many jurisdictions preview the written test in the exam announcement by including a section called "Knowledge and Abilities Required," "Scope of the Examination," or some similar heading. Here you will find out specifically what fields will be tested.

2) Review your own background

Once you learn in general what the position is all about, and what you need to know to do the work, ask yourself which subjects you already know fairly well and which need improvement. You may wonder whether to concentrate on improving your strong areas or on building some background in your fields of weakness. When the announcement has specified "some knowledge" or "considerable knowledge," or has used adjectives like "beginning principles of..." or "advanced ... methods," you can get a clue as to the number and difficulty of questions to be asked in any given field. More questions, and hence broader coverage, would be included for those subjects which are more important in the work. Now weigh your strengths and weaknesses against the job requirements and prepare accordingly.

3) Determine the level of the position

Another way to tell how intensively you should prepare is to understand the level of the job for which you are applying. Is it the entering level? In other words, is this the position in which beginners in a field of work are hired? Or is it an intermediate or advanced level? Sometimes this is indicated by such words as "Junior" or "Senior" in the class title. Other jurisdictions use Roman numerals to designate the level – Clerk I, Clerk II, for example. The word "Supervisor" sometimes appears in the title. If the level is not indicated by the title, check the description of duties. Will you be working under very close supervision, or will you have responsibility for independent decisions in this work?

4) Choose appropriate study materials

Now that you know the subjects to be examined and the relative amount of each subject to be covered, you can choose suitable study materials. For beginning level jobs, or even advanced ones, if you have a pronounced weakness in some aspect of your training, read a modern, standard textbook in that field. Be sure it is up to date and has general coverage. Such books are normally available at your library, and the librarian will be glad to help you locate one. For entry-level positions, questions of appropriate difficulty are chosen – neither highly advanced questions, nor those too simple. Such questions require careful thought but not advanced training.

If the position for which you are applying is technical or advanced, you will read more advanced, specialized material. If you are already familiar with the basic principles of your field, elementary textbooks would waste your time. Concentrate on advanced textbooks and technical periodicals. Think through the concepts and review difficult problems in your field.

These are all general sources. You can get more ideas on your own initiative, following these leads. For example, training manuals and publications of the government agency which employs workers in your field can be useful, particularly for technical and professional positions. A letter or visit to the government department involved may result in more specific study suggestions, and certainly will provide you with a more definite idea of the exact nature of the position you are seeking.

III. KINDS OF TESTS

Tests are used for purposes other than measuring knowledge and ability to perform specified duties. For some positions, it is equally important to test ability to make adjustments to new situations or to profit from training. In others, basic mental abilities not dependent on information are essential. Questions which test these things may not appear as pertinent to the duties of the position as those which test for knowledge and information. Yet they are often highly important parts of a fair examination. For very general questions, it is almost impossible to help you direct your study efforts. What we can do is to point out some of the more common of these general abilities needed in public service positions and describe some typical questions.

1) General information

Broad, general information has been found useful for predicting job success in some kinds of work. This is tested in a variety of ways, from vocabulary lists to questions about current events. Basic background in some field of work, such as sociology or economics, may be sampled in a group of questions. Often these are principles which have become familiar to most persons through exposure rather than through formal training. It is difficult to advise you how to study for these questions; being alert to the world around you is our best suggestion.

2) Verbal ability

An example of an ability needed in many positions is verbal or language ability. Verbal ability is, in brief, the ability to use and understand words. Vocabulary and grammar tests are typical measures of this ability. Reading comprehension or paragraph interpretation questions are common in many kinds of civil service tests. You are given a paragraph of written material and asked to find its central meaning.

3) Numerical ability

Number skills can be tested by the familiar arithmetic problem, by checking paired lists of numbers to see which are alike and which are different, or by interpreting charts and graphs. In the latter test, a graph may be printed in the test booklet which you are asked to use as the basis for answering questions.

4) Observation

A popular test for law-enforcement positions is the observation test. A picture is shown to you for several minutes, then taken away. Questions about the picture test your ability to observe both details and larger elements.

5) Following directions

In many positions in the public service, the employee must be able to carry out written instructions dependably and accurately. You may be given a chart with several columns, each column listing a variety of information. The questions require you to carry out directions involving the information given in the chart.

6) Skills and aptitudes

Performance tests effectively measure some manual skills and aptitudes. When the skill is one in which you are trained, such as typing or shorthand, you can practice. These tests are often very much like those given in business school or high school courses. For many of the other skills and aptitudes, however, no short-time preparation can be made. Skills and abilities natural to you or that you have developed throughout your lifetime are being tested.

Many of the general questions just described provide all the data needed to answer the questions and ask you to use your reasoning ability to find the answers. Your best preparation for these tests, as well as for tests of facts and ideas, is to be at your physical and mental best. You, no doubt, have your own methods of getting into an exam-taking mood and keeping "in shape." The next section lists some ideas on this subject.

IV. KINDS OF QUESTIONS

Only rarely is the "essay" question, which you answer in narrative form, used in civil service tests. Civil service tests are usually of the short-answer type. Full instructions for answering these questions will be given to you at the examination. But in case this is your first experience with short-answer questions and separate answer sheets, here is what you need to know:

1) Multiple-choice Questions

Most popular of the short-answer questions is the "multiple choice" or "best answer" question. It can be used, for example, to test for factual knowledge, ability to solve problems or judgment in meeting situations found at work.

A multiple-choice question is normally one of three types—
- It can begin with an incomplete statement followed by several possible endings. You are to find the one ending which *best* completes the statement, although some of the others may not be entirely wrong.
- It can also be a complete statement in the form of a question which is answered by choosing one of the statements listed.
- It can be in the form of a problem – again you select the best answer.

Here is an example of a multiple-choice question with a discussion which should give you some clues as to the method for choosing the right answer:

When an employee has a complaint about his assignment, the action which will *best* help him overcome his difficulty is to
  A. discuss his difficulty with his coworkers
  B. take the problem to the head of the organization
  C. take the problem to the person who gave him the assignment
  D. say nothing to anyone about his complaint

In answering this question, you should study each of the choices to find which is best. Consider choice "A" – Certainly an employee may discuss his complaint with fellow employees, but no change or improvement can result, and the complaint remains unresolved. Choice "B" is a poor choice since the head of the organization probably does not know what assignment you have been given, and taking your problem to him is known as "going over the head" of the supervisor. The supervisor, or person who made the assignment, is the person who can clarify it or correct any injustice. Choice "C" is, therefore, correct. To say nothing, as in choice "D," is unwise. Supervisors have and interest in knowing the problems employees are facing, and the employee is seeking a solution to his problem.

2) True/False Questions

The "true/false" or "right/wrong" form of question is sometimes used. Here a complete statement is given. Your job is to decide whether the statement is right or wrong.

SAMPLE: A roaming cell-phone call to a nearby city costs less than a non-roaming call to a distant city.

This statement is wrong, or false, since roaming calls are more expensive.
This is not a complete list of all possible question forms, although most of the others are variations of these common types. You will always get complete directions for

answering questions. Be sure you understand *how* to mark your answers – ask questions until you do.

V. RECORDING YOUR ANSWERS

Computer terminals are used more and more today for many different kinds of exams.

For an examination with very few applicants, you may be told to record your answers in the test booklet itself. Separate answer sheets are much more common. If this separate answer sheet is to be scored by machine – and this is often the case – it is highly important that you mark your answers correctly in order to get credit.

An electronic scoring machine is often used in civil service offices because of the speed with which papers can be scored. Machine-scored answer sheets must be marked with a pencil, which will be given to you. This pencil has a high graphite content which responds to the electronic scoring machine. As a matter of fact, stray dots may register as answers, so do not let your pencil rest on the answer sheet while you are pondering the correct answer. Also, if your pencil lead breaks or is otherwise defective, ask for another.

Since the answer sheet will be dropped in a slot in the scoring machine, be careful not to bend the corners or get the paper crumpled.

The answer sheet normally has five vertical columns of numbers, with 30 numbers to a column. These numbers correspond to the question numbers in your test booklet. After each number, going across the page are four or five pairs of dotted lines. These short dotted lines have small letters or numbers above them. The first two pairs may also have a "T" or "F" above the letters. This indicates that the first two pairs only are to be used if the questions are of the true-false type. If the questions are multiple choice, disregard the "T" and "F" and pay attention only to the small letters or numbers.

Answer your questions in the manner of the sample that follows:

32. The largest city in the United States is
   A. Washington, D.C.
   B. New York City
   C. Chicago
   D. Detroit
   E. San Francisco

1) Choose the answer you think is best. (New York City is the largest, so "B" is correct.)
2) Find the row of dotted lines numbered the same as the question you are answering. (Find row number 32)
3) Find the pair of dotted lines corresponding to the answer. (Find the pair of lines under the mark "B.")
4) Make a solid black mark between the dotted lines.

VI. BEFORE THE TEST

Common sense will help you find procedures to follow to get ready for an examination. Too many of us, however, overlook these sensible measures. Indeed, nervousness and fatigue have been found to be the most serious reasons why applicants fail to do their best on civil service tests. Here is a list of reminders:

- Begin your preparation early – Don't wait until the last minute to go scurrying around for books and materials or to find out what the position is all about.
- Prepare continuously – An hour a night for a week is better than an all-night cram session. This has been definitely established. What is more, a night a week for a month will return better dividends than crowding your study into a shorter period of time.
- Locate the place of the exam – You have been sent a notice telling you when and where to report for the examination. If the location is in a different town or otherwise unfamiliar to you, it would be well to inquire the best route and learn something about the building.
- Relax the night before the test – Allow your mind to rest. Do not study at all that night. Plan some mild recreation or diversion; then go to bed early and get a good night's sleep.
- Get up early enough to make a leisurely trip to the place for the test – This way unforeseen events, traffic snarls, unfamiliar buildings, etc. will not upset you.
- Dress comfortably – A written test is not a fashion show. You will be known by number and not by name, so wear something comfortable.
- Leave excess paraphernalia at home – Shopping bags and odd bundles will get in your way. You need bring only the items mentioned in the official notice you received; usually everything you need is provided. Do not bring reference books to the exam. They will only confuse those last minutes and be taken away from you when in the test room.
- Arrive somewhat ahead of time – If because of transportation schedules you must get there very early, bring a newspaper or magazine to take your mind off yourself while waiting.
- Locate the examination room – When you have found the proper room, you will be directed to the seat or part of the room where you will sit. Sometimes you are given a sheet of instructions to read while you are waiting. Do not fill out any forms until you are told to do so; just read them and be prepared.
- Relax and prepare to listen to the instructions
- If you have any physical problem that may keep you from doing your best, be sure to tell the test administrator. If you are sick or in poor health, you really cannot do your best on the exam. You can come back and take the test some other time.

VII. AT THE TEST

The day of the test is here and you have the test booklet in your hand. The temptation to get going is very strong. Caution! There is more to success than knowing the right answers. You must know how to identify your papers and understand variations in the type of short-answer question used in this particular examination. Follow these suggestions for maximum results from your efforts:

1) Cooperate with the monitor

The test administrator has a duty to create a situation in which you can be as much at ease as possible. He will give instructions, tell you when to begin, check to see that you are marking your answer sheet correctly, and so on. He is not there to guard you, although he will see that your competitors do not take unfair advantage. He wants to help you do your best.

2) Listen to all instructions

Don't jump the gun! Wait until you understand all directions. In most civil service tests you get more time than you need to answer the questions. So don't be in a hurry. Read each word of instructions until you clearly understand the meaning. Study the examples, listen to all announcements and follow directions. Ask questions if you do not understand what to do.

3) Identify your papers

Civil service exams are usually identified by number only. You will be assigned a number; you must not put your name on your test papers. Be sure to copy your number correctly. Since more than one exam may be given, copy your exact examination title.

4) Plan your time

Unless you are told that a test is a "speed" or "rate of work" test, speed itself is usually not important. Time enough to answer all the questions will be provided, but this does not mean that you have all day. An overall time limit has been set. Divide the total time (in minutes) by the number of questions to determine the approximate time you have for each question.

5) Do not linger over difficult questions

If you come across a difficult question, mark it with a paper clip (useful to have along) and come back to it when you have been through the booklet. One caution if you do this – be sure to skip a number on your answer sheet as well. Check often to be sure that you have not lost your place and that you are marking in the row numbered the same as the question you are answering.

6) Read the questions

Be sure you know what the question asks! Many capable people are unsuccessful because they failed to *read* the questions correctly.

7) Answer all questions

Unless you have been instructed that a penalty will be deducted for incorrect answers, it is better to guess than to omit a question.

8) Speed tests

It is often better NOT to guess on speed tests. It has been found that on timed tests people are tempted to spend the last few seconds before time is called in marking answers at random – without even reading them – in the hope of picking up a few extra points. To discourage this practice, the instructions may warn you that your score will be "corrected" for guessing. That is, a penalty will be applied. The incorrect answers will be deducted from the correct ones, or some other penalty formula will be used.

9) Review your answers
   If you finish before time is called, go back to the questions you guessed or omitted to give them further thought. Review other answers if you have time.

10) Return your test materials
   If you are ready to leave before others have finished or time is called, take ALL your materials to the monitor and leave quietly. Never take any test material with you. The monitor can discover whose papers are not complete, and taking a test booklet may be grounds for disqualification.

VIII. EXAMINATION TECHNIQUES

1) Read the general instructions carefully. These are usually printed on the first page of the exam booklet. As a rule, these instructions refer to the timing of the examination; the fact that you should not start work until the signal and must stop work at a signal, etc. If there are any *special* instructions, such as a choice of questions to be answered, make sure that you note this instruction carefully.

2) When you are ready to start work on the examination, that is as soon as the signal has been given, read the instructions to each question booklet, underline any key words or phrases, such as *least, best, outline, describe* and the like. In this way you will tend to answer as requested rather than discover on reviewing your paper that you *listed without describing*, that you selected the *worst* choice rather than the *best* choice, etc.

3) If the examination is of the objective or multiple-choice type – that is, each question will also give a series of possible answers: A, B, C or D, and you are called upon to select the best answer and write the letter next to that answer on your answer paper – it is advisable to start answering each question in turn. There may be anywhere from 50 to 100 such questions in the three or four hours allotted and you can see how much time would be taken if you read through all the questions before beginning to answer any. Furthermore, if you come across a question or group of questions which you know would be difficult to answer, it would undoubtedly affect your handling of all the other questions.

4) If the examination is of the essay type and contains but a few questions, it is a moot point as to whether you should read all the questions before starting to answer any one. Of course, if you are given a choice – say five out of seven and the like – then it is essential to read all the questions so you can eliminate the two that are most difficult. If, however, you are asked to answer all the questions, there may be danger in trying to answer the easiest one first because you may find that you will spend too much time on it. The best technique is to answer the first question, then proceed to the second, etc.

5) Time your answers. Before the exam begins, write down the time it started, then add the time allowed for the examination and write down the time it must be completed, then divide the time available somewhat as follows:

- If 3-1/2 hours are allowed, that would be 210 minutes. If you have 80 objective-type questions, that would be an average of 2-1/2 minutes per question. Allow yourself no more than 2 minutes per question, or a total of 160 minutes, which will permit about 50 minutes to review.
- If for the time allotment of 210 minutes there are 7 essay questions to answer, that would average about 30 minutes a question. Give yourself only 25 minutes per question so that you have about 35 minutes to review.

6) The most important instruction is to *read each question* and make sure you know what is wanted. The second most important instruction is to *time yourself properly* so that you answer every question. The third most important instruction is to *answer every question*. Guess if you have to but include something for each question. Remember that you will receive no credit for a blank and will probably receive some credit if you write something in answer to an essay question. If you guess a letter – say "B" for a multiple-choice question – you may have guessed right. If you leave a blank as an answer to a multiple-choice question, the examiners may respect your feelings but it will not add a point to your score. Some exams may penalize you for wrong answers, so in such cases *only*, you may not want to guess unless you have some basis for your answer.

7) Suggestions
   a. Objective-type questions
      1. Examine the question booklet for proper sequence of pages and questions
      2. Read all instructions carefully
      3. Skip any question which seems too difficult; return to it after all other questions have been answered
      4. Apportion your time properly; do not spend too much time on any single question or group of questions
      5. Note and underline key words – *all, most, fewest, least, best, worst, same, opposite,* etc.
      6. Pay particular attention to negatives
      7. Note unusual option, e.g., unduly long, short, complex, different or similar in content to the body of the question
      8. Observe the use of "hedging" words – *probably, may, most likely,* etc.
      9. Make sure that your answer is put next to the same number as the question
      10. Do not second-guess unless you have good reason to believe the second answer is definitely more correct
      11. Cross out original answer if you decide another answer is more accurate; do not erase until you are ready to hand your paper in
      12. Answer all questions; guess unless instructed otherwise
      13. Leave time for review

   b. Essay questions
      1. Read each question carefully
      2. Determine exactly what is wanted. Underline key words or phrases.
      3. Decide on outline or paragraph answer

4. Include many different points and elements unless asked to develop any one or two points or elements
5. Show impartiality by giving pros and cons unless directed to select one side only
6. Make and write down any assumptions you find necessary to answer the questions
7. Watch your English, grammar, punctuation and choice of words
8. Time your answers; don't crowd material

8) Answering the essay question

Most essay questions can be answered by framing the specific response around several key words or ideas. Here are a few such key words or ideas:

M's: manpower, materials, methods, money, management
P's: purpose, program, policy, plan, procedure, practice, problems, pitfalls, personnel, public relations

  a. Six basic steps in handling problems:
    1. Preliminary plan and background development
    2. Collect information, data and facts
    3. Analyze and interpret information, data and facts
    4. Analyze and develop solutions as well as make recommendations
    5. Prepare report and sell recommendations
    6. Install recommendations and follow up effectiveness

  b. Pitfalls to avoid
    1. *Taking things for granted* – A statement of the situation does not necessarily imply that each of the elements is necessarily true; for example, a complaint may be invalid and biased so that all that can be taken for granted is that a complaint has been registered
    2. *Considering only one side of a situation* – Wherever possible, indicate several alternatives and then point out the reasons you selected the best one
    3. *Failing to indicate follow up* – Whenever your answer indicates action on your part, make certain that you will take proper follow-up action to see how successful your recommendations, procedures or actions turn out to be
    4. *Taking too long in answering any single question* – Remember to time your answers properly

IX. AFTER THE TEST

Scoring procedures differ in detail among civil service jurisdictions although the general principles are the same. Whether the papers are hand-scored or graded by machine we have described, they are nearly always graded by number. That is, the person who marks the paper knows only the number – never the name – of the applicant. Not until all the papers have been graded will they be matched with names. If other tests, such as training and experience or oral interview ratings have been given, scores will be combined. Different parts of the examination usually have different weights. For example, the written test might count 60 percent of the final grade, and a rating of training and experience 40 percent. In many jurisdictions, veterans will have a certain number of points added to their grades.

After the final grade has been determined, the names are placed in grade order and an eligible list is established. There are various methods for resolving ties between those who get the same final grade – probably the most common is to place first the name of the person whose application was received first. Job offers are made from the eligible list in the order the names appear on it. You will be notified of your grade and your rank as soon as all these computations have been made. This will be done as rapidly as possible.

People who are found to meet the requirements in the announcement are called "eligibles." Their names are put on a list of eligible candidates. An eligible's chances of getting a job depend on how high he stands on this list and how fast agencies are filling jobs from the list.

When a job is to be filled from a list of eligibles, the agency asks for the names of people on the list of eligibles for that job. When the civil service commission receives this request, it sends to the agency the names of the three people highest on this list. Or, if the job to be filled has specialized requirements, the office sends the agency the names of the top three persons who meet these requirements from the general list.

The appointing officer makes a choice from among the three people whose names were sent to him. If the selected person accepts the appointment, the names of the others are put back on the list to be considered for future openings.

That is the rule in hiring from all kinds of eligible lists, whether they are for typist, carpenter, chemist, or something else. For every vacancy, the appointing officer has his choice of any one of the top three eligibles on the list. This explains why the person whose name is on top of the list sometimes does not get an appointment when some of the persons lower on the list do. If the appointing officer chooses the second or third eligible, the No. 1 eligible does not get a job at once, but stays on the list until he is appointed or the list is terminated.

X. HOW TO PASS THE INTERVIEW TEST

The examination for which you applied requires an oral interview test. You have already taken the written test and you are now being called for the interview test – the final part of the formal examination.

You may think that it is not possible to prepare for an interview test and that there are no procedures to follow during an interview. Our purpose is to point out some things you can do in advance that will help you and some good rules to follow and pitfalls to avoid while you are being interviewed.

What is an interview supposed to test?

The written examination is designed to test the technical knowledge and competence of the candidate; the oral is designed to evaluate intangible qualities, not readily measured otherwise, and to establish a list showing the relative fitness of each candidate – as measured against his competitors – for the position sought. Scoring is not on the basis of "right" and "wrong," but on a sliding scale of values ranging from "not passable" to "outstanding." As a matter of fact, it is possible to achieve a relatively low score without a single "incorrect" answer because of evident weakness in the qualities being measured.

Occasionally, an examination may consist entirely of an oral test – either an individual or a group oral. In such cases, information is sought concerning the technical knowledges and abilities of the candidate, since there has been no written examination for this purpose. More commonly, however, an oral test is used to supplement a written examination.

Who conducts interviews?
The composition of oral boards varies among different jurisdictions. In nearly all, a representative of the personnel department serves as chairman. One of the members of the board may be a representative of the department in which the candidate would work. In some cases, "outside experts" are used, and, frequently, a businessman or some other representative of the general public is asked to serve. Labor and management or other special groups may be represented. The aim is to secure the services of experts in the appropriate field.

However the board is composed, it is a good idea (and not at all improper or unethical) to ascertain in advance of the interview who the members are and what groups they represent. When you are introduced to them, you will have some idea of their backgrounds and interests, and at least you will not stutter and stammer over their names.

What should be done before the interview?
While knowledge about the board members is useful and takes some of the surprise element out of the interview, there is other preparation which is more substantive. It *is* possible to prepare for an oral interview – in several ways:

1) Keep a copy of your application and review it carefully before the interview
This may be the only document before the oral board, and the starting point of the interview. Know what education and experience you have listed there, and the sequence and dates of all of it. Sometimes the board will ask you to review the highlights of your experience for them; you should not have to hem and haw doing it.

2) Study the class specification and the examination announcement
Usually, the oral board has one or both of these to guide them. The qualities, characteristics or knowledges required by the position sought are stated in these documents. They offer valuable clues as to the nature of the oral interview. For example, if the job involves supervisory responsibilities, the announcement will usually indicate that knowledge of modern supervisory methods and the qualifications of the candidate as a supervisor will be tested. If so, you can expect such questions, frequently in the form of a hypothetical situation which you are expected to solve. NEVER go into an oral without knowledge of the duties and responsibilities of the job you seek.

3) Think through each qualification required
Try to visualize the kind of questions you would ask if you were a board member. How well could you answer them? Try especially to appraise your own knowledge and background in each area, *measured against the job sought*, and identify any areas in which you are weak. Be critical and realistic – do not flatter yourself.

4) Do some general reading in areas in which you feel you may be weak
For example, if the job involves supervision and your past experience has NOT, some general reading in supervisory methods and practices, particularly in the field of human relations, might be useful. Do NOT study agency procedures or detailed manuals. The oral board will be testing your understanding and capacity, not your memory.

5) Get a good night's sleep and watch your general health and mental attitude
You will want a clear head at the interview. Take care of a cold or any other minor ailment, and of course, no hangovers.

What should be done on the day of the interview?
Now comes the day of the interview itself. Give yourself plenty of time to get there. Plan to arrive somewhat ahead of the scheduled time, particularly if your appointment is in the fore part of the day. If a previous candidate fails to appear, the board might be ready for you a bit early. By early afternoon an oral board is almost invariably behind schedule if there are many candidates, and you may have to wait. Take along a book or magazine to read, or your application to review, but leave any extraneous material in the waiting room when you go in for your interview. In any event, relax and compose yourself.

The matter of dress is important. The board is forming impressions about you – from your experience, your manners, your attitude, and your appearance. Give your personal appearance careful attention. Dress your best, but not your flashiest. Choose conservative, appropriate clothing, and be sure it is immaculate. This is a business interview, and your appearance should indicate that you regard it as such. Besides, being well groomed and properly dressed will help boost your confidence.

Sooner or later, someone will call your name and escort you into the interview room. *This is it.* From here on you are on your own. It is too late for any more preparation. But remember, you asked for this opportunity to prove your fitness, and you are here because your request was granted.

What happens when you go in?
The usual sequence of events will be as follows: The clerk (who is often the board stenographer) will introduce you to the chairman of the oral board, who will introduce you to the other members of the board. Acknowledge the introductions before you sit down. Do not be surprised if you find a microphone facing you or a stenotypist sitting by. Oral interviews are usually recorded in the event of an appeal or other review.

Usually the chairman of the board will open the interview by reviewing the highlights of your education and work experience from your application – primarily for the benefit of the other members of the board, as well as to get the material into the record. Do not interrupt or comment unless there is an error or significant misinterpretation; if that is the case, do not hesitate. But do not quibble about insignificant matters. Also, he will usually ask you some question about your education, experience or your present job – partly to get you to start talking and to establish the interviewing "rapport." He may start the actual questioning, or turn it over to one of the other members. Frequently, each member undertakes the questioning on a particular area, one in which he is perhaps most competent, so you can expect each member to participate in the examination. Because time is limited, you may also expect some rather abrupt switches in the direction the questioning takes, so do not be upset by it. Normally, a board member will not pursue a single line of questioning unless he discovers a particular strength or weakness.

After each member has participated, the chairman will usually ask whether any member has any further questions, then will ask you if you have anything you wish to add. Unless you are expecting this question, it may floor you. Worse, it may start you off on an extended, extemporaneous speech. The board is not usually seeking more information. The question is principally to offer you a last opportunity to present further qualifications or to indicate that you have nothing to add. So, if you feel that a significant qualification or characteristic has been overlooked, it is proper to point it out in a sentence or so. Do not compliment the board on the thoroughness of their examination – they have been sketchy, and you know it. If you wish, merely say, "No thank you, I have nothing further to add." This is a point where you can "talk yourself out" of a good impression or fail to present an important bit of information. Remember, *you close the interview yourself.*

The chairman will then say, "That is all, Mr. _____, thank you." Do not be startled; the interview is over, and quicker than you think. Thank him, gather your belongings and take your leave. Save your sigh of relief for the other side of the door.

How to put your best foot forward

Throughout this entire process, you may feel that the board individually and collectively is trying to pierce your defenses, seek out your hidden weaknesses and embarrass and confuse you. Actually, this is not true. They are obliged to make an appraisal of your qualifications for the job you are seeking, and they want to see you in your best light. Remember, they must interview all candidates and a non-cooperative candidate may become a failure in spite of their best efforts to bring out his qualifications. Here are 15 suggestions that will help you:

1) Be natural – Keep your attitude confident, not cocky

If you are not confident that you can do the job, do not expect the board to be. Do not apologize for your weaknesses, try to bring out your strong points. The board is interested in a positive, not negative, presentation. Cockiness will antagonize any board member and make him wonder if you are covering up a weakness by a false show of strength.

2) Get comfortable, but don't lounge or sprawl

Sit erectly but not stiffly. A careless posture may lead the board to conclude that you are careless in other things, or at least that you are not impressed by the importance of the occasion. Either conclusion is natural, even if incorrect. Do not fuss with your clothing, a pencil or an ashtray. Your hands may occasionally be useful to emphasize a point; do not let them become a point of distraction.

3) Do not wisecrack or make small talk

This is a serious situation, and your attitude should show that you consider it as such. Further, the time of the board is limited – they do not want to waste it, and neither should you.

4) Do not exaggerate your experience or abilities

In the first place, from information in the application or other interviews and sources, the board may know more about you than you think. Secondly, you probably will not get away with it. An experienced board is rather adept at spotting such a situation, so do not take the chance.

5) If you know a board member, do not make a point of it, yet do not hide it

Certainly you are not fooling him, and probably not the other members of the board. Do not try to take advantage of your acquaintanceship – it will probably do you little good.

6) Do not dominate the interview

Let the board do that. They will give you the clues – do not assume that you have to do all the talking. Realize that the board has a number of questions to ask you, and do not try to take up all the interview time by showing off your extensive knowledge of the answer to the first one.

7) Be attentive

You only have 20 minutes or so, and you should keep your attention at its sharpest throughout. When a member is addressing a problem or question to you, give him your undivided attention. Address your reply principally to him, but do not exclude the other board members.

8) Do not interrupt

A board member may be stating a problem for you to analyze. He will ask you a question when the time comes. Let him state the problem, and wait for the question.

9) Make sure you understand the question

Do not try to answer until you are sure what the question is. If it is not clear, restate it in your own words or ask the board member to clarify it for you. However, do not haggle about minor elements.

10) Reply promptly but not hastily

A common entry on oral board rating sheets is "candidate responded readily," or "candidate hesitated in replies." Respond as promptly and quickly as you can, but do not jump to a hasty, ill-considered answer.

11) Do not be peremptory in your answers

A brief answer is proper – but do not fire your answer back. That is a losing game from your point of view. The board member can probably ask questions much faster than you can answer them.

12) Do not try to create the answer you think the board member wants

He is interested in what kind of mind you have and how it works – not in playing games. Furthermore, he can usually spot this practice and will actually grade you down on it.

13) Do not switch sides in your reply merely to agree with a board member

Frequently, a member will take a contrary position merely to draw you out and to see if you are willing and able to defend your point of view. Do not start a debate, yet do not surrender a good position. If a position is worth taking, it is worth defending.

14) Do not be afraid to admit an error in judgment if you are shown to be wrong

The board knows that you are forced to reply without any opportunity for careful consideration. Your answer may be demonstrably wrong. If so, admit it and get on with the interview.

15) Do not dwell at length on your present job

The opening question may relate to your present assignment. Answer the question but do not go into an extended discussion. You are being examined for a *new* job, not your present one. As a matter of fact, try to phrase ALL your answers in terms of the job for which you are being examined.

Basis of Rating

Probably you will forget most of these "do's" and "don'ts" when you walk into the oral interview room. Even remembering them all will not ensure you a passing grade. Perhaps you did not have the qualifications in the first place. But remembering them will help you to put your best foot forward, without treading on the toes of the board members.

Rumor and popular opinion to the contrary notwithstanding, an oral board wants you to make the best appearance possible. They know you are under pressure – but they also want to see how you respond to it as a guide to what your reaction would be under the pressures of the job you seek. They will be influenced by the degree of poise you display, the personal traits you show and the manner in which you respond.

ABOUT THIS BOOK

This book contains tests divided into Examination Sections. Go through each test, answering every question in the margin. At the end of each test look at the answer key and check your answers. On the ones you got wrong, look at the right answer choice and learn. Do not fill in the answers first. Do not memorize the questions and answers, but understand the answer and principles involved. On your test, the questions will likely be different from the samples. Questions are changed and new ones added. If you understand these past questions you should have success with any changes that arise. Tests may consist of several types of questions. We have additional books on each subject should more study be advisable or necessary for you. Finally, the more you study, the better prepared you will be. This book is intended to be the last thing you study before you walk into the examination room. Prior study of relevant texts is also recommended. NLC publishes some of these in our Fundamental Series. Knowledge and good sense are important factors in passing your exam. Good luck also helps. So now study this Passbook, absorb the material contained within and take that knowledge into the examination. Then do your best to pass that exam.

EXAMINATION SECTION

EXAMINATION SECTION
TEST 1

DIRECTIONS: Each question or incomplete statement is followed by several suggested answers or completions. Select the one that BEST answers the question or completes the statement. *PRINT THE LETTER OF THE CORRECT ANSWER IN THE SPACE AT THE RIGHT.*

1. There is a calendar of dates pertinent to the procedures for seeking an assessment reduction in the city.
   The one of the following statements which does NOT present an accurate date in the procedure is

   A. tax books are open to the public on February 1
   B. the protest period begins on February 1 and ends on March 15
   C. the final assessment roll is published on May 25
   D. the last day on which to institute a Note of Issue hearing is October 24

   1._____

2. Technical assistants should be consulted by assessors on various aspects of the assessors' responsibilities.
   The one of the following tasks on which an assessor need NOT consult with his technical assistant is that of

   A. determining unit costs for various types of construction
   B. recording all relevant appraisal data in the field book
   C. obtaining pertinent information from the city record and the board calendars and resolutions
   D. making significant changes in the valuation of specific parcels

   2._____

3. To achieve equality in assessment and equalization of units of value, the assessor must at regular intervals seek the advice of others.
   The one of the following with whom the assessor does NOT have to confer on this problem is

   A. his technical assistant
   B. the assessor of an adjoining district
   C. the assessor of an adjoining district in another borough
   D. the borough tax commissioner

   3._____

4. A parcel in an exempt status on the current assessment roll has just been purchased by a commercial business. Upon learning of this change in ownership, which one of the following is the CORRECT action for the assessor to take?

   A. Refer the matter to the tax commissioner for a final decision.
   B. Grant the exemption on his own pursuant to statute and local law.
   C. Refer the matter to the assessor-in-charge for a final decision.
   D. Refer the matter to the technical assistant for a final decision.

   4._____

5. A veteran who owns a home in which he has a veteran's exemption of $4,000 wishes to sell this home and purchase a larger home. He visits the borough office of the real property assessment department and asks advice from you on how to proceed.
   Which one of the following would be INCORRECT counsel?

   5._____

A. The purchase of the new home should be made prior to tax status day and exemption papers should be filed between February 1 and March 15 for the exemption to be effective for the ensuing year.
B. Since this veteran had not reached the maximum amount of eligible funds, he should furnish evidence of the receipt and inclusion of any additional eligible funds in the purchase of the new home.
C. If the veteran sells his present home before he buys his new home, he will be able to transfer his veteran's exemption to the new home.
D. As long as his present home is sold and the new home is purchased, both occurring prior to tax status day, it is immaterial which transaction takes place first.

6. In reviewing an assessor's report for certiorari proceedings, you note that the current assessed valuation for the property is $325,000 and the net income for the property is $39,000.
The % Net on A.V. required on the form is

   A. not determinable from the data given
   B. 7.5%
   C. 8.333%
   D. 12%

7. The individual assessments in a condominium development are finalized by the

   A. assessor-in-charge of the borough
   B. senior assessor
   C. research bureau
   D. bureau of equalization

8. A property is exempt from real estate taxation because it is owned by a religious institution. During the course of your field inspections, you observe that a new building has been constructed adjacent to the existing structure on the same tax lot.
As a supervisor, you are required to

   A. assess the property, including the new improvement, such that the full increased valuation is exempt
   B. report this on a query sheet, for referral to the tax commissioner, who will determine whether the property is to be restored to the tax rolls
   C. advise the research bureau, which will make a cost analysis of the new building
   D. check to see whether the owner has filed the appropriate form

9. Three years ago, an exemption privilege was granted to a real property whose owner was over 65 years of age and had limited income. The property was sold on March 20, 2006 to a 57-year-old Vietnam War veteran. With regard to the eligibility for exemption of this property, it is CORRECT to state that

   A. since the assessment period runs from July 1 to June 30, the exemption privilege will remain until June 30
   B. when the property is sold, it is immediately restored to taxable status and the exemption privilege ceases
   C. since taxable status date is January 25, the exemption privilege will remain until that date
   D. since the veteran is eligible for exemption, the property may retain its exemption until he files an application for exemption during the 2007 protest period

10. An assessor in one of your districts has made a study which indicates that market value has risen and, therefore, he believes that assessed valuations should be accordingly increased.
    As supervisor, it is your responsibility to

    A. make an intensive review of his data and if it confirms a market-level increase, advise him to increase assessed valuations by the same percentage of increase as the market indicates
    B. insist that any market-level increase be supported by paired sales and if these sales indicate that increase, raise assessed values accordingly
    C. review his proposed tenative assessments with the assessor and if you note unusual increases as compared with the previous assessments, consult with the assessor-in-charge
    D. advise the assessor to increase assessed valuations moderately at a much lower percentage increase than the market indicates

11. The application for correction of assessed valuation of real estate requires that rental income and expenses be listed for the calendar year or the applicant's fiscal year. In listing his income and expense data, the applicant MUST include all

    A. income received or accrued during the period and all expenses paid or incurred during the period except for insurance, which is prorated for the period covered
    B. income received or accrued during the period and all expenses paid or incurred during the period on a non-prorated basis
    C. rentals as if the building were fully occupied without regard to vacancies and all expenses paid or incurred during the period
    D. income actually collected during the period and all expenses prorated on an annual basis

12. The date on which the finance administrator shall submit to the mayor, the board of estimate, and the city council a tentative estimate of the assessed valuation of real property subject to taxation for the ensuing fiscal year is

    A. January 1   B. March 1   C. May 1   D. July 1

13. An assessor, during the course of his annual inspection, notes that the ownership of an exempt property has changed during the last year.
    The assessor is required to

    A. refer this fact to the tax commission for appropriate action
    B. advise the new owner that unless he meets the same qualifications as the previous owner, the exemption will be cancelled
    C. make investigation as to the date the new owner acquired title and cancel the exemption as of that date
    D. prepare a query sheet for submission to the research bureau which will make all investigations as to the new ownership

14. Assessors are required to make annual inspections of exempt properties to determine the name of owner, use and occupancy.
    In regard to partially exempt properties, assessors must pay particular attention to

A. investigating whether title is held in an individual or corporate name
B. assessing the property on a different basis from that on which a wholly exempt property is assessed
C. ascertaining whether a certificate of occupancy has been issued for the current use and purpose for which the exemption was granted
D. assessing the property on a different basis from that on which a property which has no exemption is assessed

15. In preparing the assessor's report for certiorari hearing, you are required to indicate all sales of subject property. In reviewing the latest sale, you discover that state stamps in the amount of $33 are affixed to the deed. You also know that the property was purchased subject to an existing mortgage of $27,000, and that the seller took back a purchase money mortgage of $25,000.
The INDICATED consideration for this property is

   A. $52,000   B. $57,000   C. $60,000   D. $82,000

16. The rule of law which resulted from the State Court of Appeals decision in the case of *Ed Guth Realty Co. v. Commissioner of Assessment of the City of Syracuse* states that

   A. application of the State equalization rate may be used as the sole basis for the ratio between assessed valuation and full valuation for tax years commencing with 1970-1971
   B. the State equalization rate has no validity in determining the ratio between assessed valuation and full valuation within a taxing district
   C. the State equalization rate can be introduced as evidence of the ratio between assessed valuation and full valuation only where the selected parcel method has also been introduced as evidence
   D. actual sales of real property within the assessing unit that occurred during the year in which the assessment under review was made are the most valid evidence of the ratio between assessed valuation and full valuation

17. Which of the following is the rule of law that resulted from the decision in the case of *People ex rel. Gale v. Tax Commission of the City of New York*?

   A. The statutory test in determining whether property is real property for tax purposes is moveability and not the intent of the owner.
   B. In arriving at full value, for tax assessment purposes, of real property subject to a lease, an appraisal is
   C. to be made of the property as a whole as if unencumbered by any lease.
   D. In determining market value of real property for tax purposes, every element which can reasonably affect the value of the property ought to be considered.
   E. It is presumed that the assessed value appearing on the assessment roll is valid and the taxpayer must carry the burden of proving the assessment invalid.

18. In relation to judidical review of assessment, the one of the following which is an INCORRECT interpretation of the State Real Property Tax Law is that

   A. a taxpayer is entitled to have his assessment reviewed only in the event the total assessment exceeds combined valuations of land and improvements
   B. there must be an affirmative showing that the land without improvements is overvalued above the total figure appearing in the assessment roll because it is only the total that may be reviewed and not the method used to derive it

C. valuation for land, a valuation for the improvements on the land, if any, and a total valuation for each separately assessed parcel within the taxing district are required
D. if the property owner concedes that the total valuation of his parcel is correct, then it is immaterial that the assessor has valued his land too low or the improvement too high

19. There is no exclusive method for valuing real property for tax assessment purposes. Which one of the following is the very BEST method for determining valuation for tax assessment purposes according to State court decisions?

    A. The cost of constructing the improvement less accrued depreciation, plus the value of the land
    B. The capitalization of the actual income of the property
    C. Comparative sales, if adjusted for the time of the sale and distance from subject property
    D. The actual sale of subject realty at arm's length if the sale is recent in time and not explained away as abnormal in any fashion

19.____

20. At the time the tax books are opened for inspection, an owner discovers that his new building, which is under construction, has been assessed for both land and improvements. The owner files an application for correction of assessed valuation on February 10, alleging that the building is under construction and will not be ready for occupancy until after April 15, and he requests the removal of the improvement assessment. On receipt of this application, the assessor inspects the building.
If he finds that it is not complete and ready for occupancy by April 15, he should

    A. eliminate the improvement assessment
    B. estimate the percentage of completion and make a partial assessment of the improvement
    C. remove the entire assessment for land and improvement
    D. remove the improvement assessment and give the land assessment a discount

20.____

21. Assume that an office building in the city is presently producing no income or is producing an income which does not show an adequate return on its total replacement cost. Which one of the following principles of valuation should be applied in arriving at an assessed value of this property?

    A. Assessors are not required to make their assessments conform rigidly to an unprofitable use of real estate by a taxpayer.
    B. The property must be assessed solely on the basis of its reproduction costs less depreciation.
    C. The assessment should be based solely on its land value with no assessment given on the improvement.
    D. A capitalization of the actual rental income of the improvement should be made, and the value so established added to the land value.

21.____

22. Under special circumstances, income from a building using a property may be considered for real estate valuation purposes.
In which of the following situations is the assessor NOT allowed to use the income produced in determining the assessed value of the property? The owner of

22.____

A. the property operates a coffee shop on premises and earns an income of $10,000 a year from the business
B. the property operates a coffee shop on the premises using 2,500 sq. ft. of rentable space. Fair market rent would be $10,000 annually.
C. an apartment house rents parking spaces to tenants for an annual income of $10,000
D. an apartment house provides coin-operated automatic washers and dryers for use of tenants. Income realized is $10,000 annually.

23. Pursuant to local law, real property owned by certain types of non-profit organizations heretofore exempt from real property taxation are now taxable.
Which one of the following properties is now subject to taxation by the city? 23.____

A. A private high school
B. The World Trade Center
C. A cemetery
D. An infirmary

24. A prospective purchaser is offered two vacant parcels, each 30,000 square feet in area, and both suitable for office buildings. Parcel 1 is zoned C6-4, with an FAR of 12 times, inclusive of bonuses. Parcel 2 is zoned C5-3, with an FAR of 18 times, inclusive of bonuses.
If it is established that Parcel 1 has a market value of $360,000, which of the following would be the APPROPRIATE market value for Parcel 2? 24.____

A. $480,000   B. $540,000   C. $630,000   D. $720,000

25. Under the administrative code, partial tax exemptions are CUSTOMARILY granted for periods of _____ years. 25.____

A. 9   B. 10   C. 12   D. 15

KEY (CORRECT ANSWERS)

1. D		11. A	
2. B		12. B	
3. D		13. A	
4. A		14. C	
5. D		15. B	
6. D		16. A	
7. C		17. B	
8. B		18. C	
9. B		19. D	
10. C		20. A	

21. A
22. A
23. D
24. B
25. C

TEST 2

DIRECTIONS: Each question or incomplete statement is followed by several suggested answers or completions. Select the one that BEST answers the question or completes the statement. *PRINT THE LETTER OF THE CORRECT ANSWER IN THE SPACE AT THE RIGHT.*

1. The MAXIMUM allowable floor area bonus available to a builder whose property is located in an R-10 zone is

    A. 5%   B. 10%   C. 20%   D. 25%

2. You have been asked to review an application for correction of assessed valuation of real estate. The applicant alleges *errors by reason of over-evaluation.*
   To prove his case, in accordance with the real property tax law, he must prove that the assessed valuation

    A. forces him to pay a real estate tax that is excessively high in relation to the rental income he receives
    B. is greater than that of a similar property in your district
    C. is greater than the full value of the property and indicate the extent of such over-valuation
    D. is illegal because of the type and occupancy of his property

3. A 67-year-old husband who is otherwise eligible applies for a senior citizen exemption on February 2, 2007. He informs the supervisor that he owned the subject house the past twenty years together with his wife as tenants by the entirety and that on her death on January 1, 2007, the ownership passed to him by descent. Her will has not yet been probated.
   Which of the following represents the counsel the supervisor should give the husband?

    A. He must wait 60 months from the time ownership passed to him before he can apply for the exemption.
    B. Title does not pass to the husband until the will has been probated, and his eligibility for exemption begins 60 months from that date.
    C. Since title to real property vests at the date of decedent's death, the husband will be eligible for exemption on December 31, 2011.
    D. He is now eligible for the senior citizen exemption and should file between February 1 and March 15.

4. A duly ordained member of the clergy who is engaged in work assigned to him by the church or denomination of which he is a member owns real property in the state and pursuant to the real property tax law may be entitled to a tax exemption.
   Which one of the following statements is MOST valid in regard to this exemption?

    A. The clergyman is entitled to the exemption regardless of the state in which he resides.
    B. A clergyman otherwise qualified loses the exemption if he has leased the property to someone not in the ministry.
    C. If a clergyman qualifies for this exemption and also qualifies for a veteran's exemption, he may claim both.
    D. A clergyman who owns real property in the city is not barred from this exemption because the work assigned to him by his denomination takes place outside the city.

2 (#2)

5. Pursuant to the real property tax law, real property purchased by a veteran is exempt from the general municipal tax to the extent that certain eligible funds were used in the purchase up to the amount of $50,000, if the veteran is not paraplegic.
The one of the following that would be considered an eligible fund is

   A. pension funds paid to a veteran by a state other than this state
   B. monthly disability payments made by the Veterans Administration to a veteran for a non-service-connected disability
   C. dependency allotment payments made while the veteran was still in service
   D. money received as repayment of a loan of mustering out pay

6. An owner relinquishes today certain rights in land for a period of twelve years during which he will receive an annual rent. Twelve years from now, the land will revert back to the owner. An appraiser seeks to estimate the current value of the reversion of the land by use of an interest table. Which one of the following tables should he select?

   A. Future worth of $1
   B. Present worth of $1
   C. Future worth of $1 per annum
   D. Present worth of $1 per annum

7. A lease provides for payment of a rental of $5,000 annually for twenty years. Assume that the interest rate is 6%.
The following factors are known:
   I. The future worth of $1 = $3.2071
   II. The present worth of $1 = $.311805
   III. The future worth of $1 per annum = $38.9927
   IV. The present worth of $1 per annum = $11.470
The value of the aforementioned lease is

   A. $1,559.03   B. $16,035.50   C. $57,350.00   D. $194,063.50

8. Assume that the capitalization of net income of an improvement exceeds its reproduction costs less depreciation.
Which of the following is an INCORRECT guideline to assessors in determining valuation in this situation?

   A. Reproduction cost less depreciation represents the maximum assessment in the absence of special circumstances.
   B. Capitalization of fair market rental of an improvement is the surest guide to a sound appraisal of the value of the realty for tax purposes.
   C. Reproduction cost less depreciation is the upper limit on an assessment of an improvement on land.
   D. In valuing improvements to realty for tax purposes, while capitalization may be considered, it may not, except in unusual circumstances, exceed the reproduction costs of the improvement less depreciation.

9. The effective gross income of an apartment house is $240,000, and allowable operating expenses exclusive of taxes amount to $70,000. The tax rate is $14.00 per $100.00 of full valuation and the taxing district assesses at 50% of full value. A purchaser seeks a 10% return including recapture.
Using the property residual method of valuation, which of the following full valuations would produce a 10% return to the purchaser?

| A. $500,000 | B. $850,000 | C. $1,000,000 | D. $1,700,000 |

10. Competent appraisers have reported that a group of 3-bedroom, 7-room homes with one bathroom, built in 1965, sell for $100,000 less than comparably built homes with two baths for which there is a stronger demand.
    The term which you would use to describe this difference in value is

    A. physical deterioration
    B. functional obsolescence
    C. economic obsolescence
    D. observed wear and tear

11. Which of the following is NOT allowable as an operating expense in deriving the net income of an income-producing property?

    A. Structural maintenance
    B. Franchise taxes
    C. Mortgage interest and amortization
    D. Management

12. Value of real property is estimated through the cost approach by

    A. analyzing sales of similar properties
    B. obtaining sales prices of new buildings and deducting estimated depreciation to determine the value of subject property
    C. ascertaining cost of acquiring similar properties including closing costs
    D. computing depreciated reproduction cost of improvements to which land value is added

13. The yield of real estate investment can be determined ONLY when

    A. the property is sold
    B. there is a net income
    C. the fiscal year is concluded
    D. there is a profit realized

14. Assume that you are examining the closing statement of a sale. The closing took place on October 15. You notice an adjustment for mortgage interest payment of $150 credited to the seller and charged to the purchaser. This should indicate to you that

    A. the seller paid the mortgagee $300 on October 1 for interest for the month of October and, therefore, the purchaser must reimburse him for half the amount
    B. this must be an error, as mortgage interest is not due until the end of the month and, therefore, the seller should be charged $150 for credit to the buyer
    C. the interest adjustment, which is treated as fire insurance premiums and taxes, was prepaid
    D. an error has been made in that interest payments should not be included in the closing statement because they are handled by the lender

15. An apartment house has a gross room rental income of $70,000 and a gross garage rental income of $11,000. The laundromat and vending machine contract provides for an income of $2,800. The reserve for vacancies is 3%.
    The effective GROSS income of the property is

    A. $81,370   B. $81,700   C. $82,500   D. $83,800

16. It may be useful for you to conduct periodic interviews with each of your subordinates to discuss his job performance in broad perspective.
    All of the following are ground rules to follow during such an interview EXCEPT

    A. showing him how he compares in work performance with other assessors in your district
    B. giving him a chance to talk
    C. focusing on what can be learned from any mistakes discussed rather than on the mistakes themselves
    D. avoiding a discussion of personalities

17. When you are correcting the errors of an assessor in your district, which of the following is NOT a good point to keep in mind?

    A. Find something on which to compliment the assessor before you correct him.
    B. Watch yourself carefully to avoid the mistake of overcorrecting.
    C. Correct the assessor at the same time as you correct other assessors who make similar mistakes.
    D. Induce the assessor to correct himself if possible.

18. Safety-mindedness cannot be achieved by command; it must be developed. Assume that you will be responsible for informing and training your subordinates in proper safety procedures.
    Which of the following methods is the MOST effective means of developing proper concern for safety among your subordinates?

    A. Award prizes for the best safety slogans
    B. Issue monthly safety bulletins
    C. Establish a safety suggestion program
    D. Hold periodic, informal group meetings on safety

19. Following are four steps to be used when instructing a subordinate in the performance of his job:
    I. Observe the subordinate doing the job
    II. Compare his performance to established standards
    III. Explain the purpose of the job to the subordinate
    IV. Demonstrate each step of the job

    Which of the following choices lists the CORRECT order in which the above steps should be taken?

    A. III, IV, I, II
    B. IV, III, I, II
    C. III, IV, II, I
    D. IV, III, II, I

20. Of the following leadership characteristics, the one that is generally considered PRIMARY for a supervisor is the ability to

    A. achieve good working relations with fellow supervisors
    B. get subordinates to air their personal problems
    C. take action to get the job done
    D. plan his work efficiently

21. A recently appointed supervisor is placed in charge of a district which includes several senior employees. He finds that while these subordinates are able to learn new tasks and methods, some of them tend to take longer to learn procedural changes than newer, younger workers.
Of the following, the MAIN reason for this is that senior workers

    A. are embarrassed by younger workers' intelligence
    B. have to *unlearn* what was taught them in the past
    C. form learning blocks when they are supervised by a younger person
    D. are more interested in doing the work than in academic discussion

22. The MAIN purpose for a supervisor's questioning the assessors at a conference he is holding is to

    A. stress those areas of information covered but not understood by the participants
    B. encourage participants to think through the problem under discussion
    C. catch those subordinates who are not paying attention
    D. permit the more knowledgeable participants to display their grasp of the problem being discussed

23. Which of the following is generally considered to be the MOST desirable way for a supervisor to begin a discussion of an employee's performance with the employee?

    A. Accentuate the positive by giving credit where credit is due
    B. Encourage the employee to suggest ways in which he can improve
    C. Point out specific instances of poor performance
    D. Suggest training programs that the employee may be interested in

24. For a supervisor to use consultative supervision with his subordinates effectively, it is ESSENTIAL that he

    A. accept the fact that his formal authority will be weakened by the procedure
    B. admit that he does not know more than all his men together and that his ideas are not always best
    C. utilize a committee system so that the procedure is orderly
    D. make sure that all subordinates are consulted so that no one feels left out

25. As a supervisor, you learn that an assessor is being transferred into your district. Another supervisor, who supervised the assessor some years ago, mentions to you that the assessor was immature, lacked confidence and concentration, and tended to panic under stress.
Of the following, the BEST action for you to take is to

    A. inform the assessor-in-charge of your borough that you do not wish the assessor transferred to your district
    B. tell the assessor when he reports for work that you know of his past problems but will help him as much as you can
    C. assign your most competent and stable assessor to work with the new employee during an orientation period
    D. observe the assessor's work to determine his current level of maturity and the type of work he can best perform

KEY (CORRECT ANSWERS)

1.	C	11.	C
2.	C	12.	D
3.	D	13.	A
4.	D	14.	B
5.	B	15.	A
6.	B	16.	A
7.	C	17.	C
8.	B	18.	D
9.	C	19.	A
10.	B	20.	C

21. B
22. B
23. A
24. D
25. D

EXAMINATION SECTION
TEST 1

DIRECTIONS: Each question or incomplete statement is followed by several suggested answers or completions. Select the one that BEST answers the question or completes the statement. PRINT THE LETTER OF THE CORRECT ANSWER IN THE SPACE AT THE RIGHT.

1. Gross income of a property less vacancy and bad debt allowance is known as

    A. net operating income
    B. contract rent
    C. gross rental profit
    D. effective gross income

2. All other factors being the same, as the neighborhood in which an income property is located deteriorates, the capitalization rate used for the property will be

    A. higher   B. lower   C. unstable   D. less reliable

3. The present cost to reproduce a shopping center, less depreciation and including the value of the land, is $2 million. An economic analysis of the income yield indicates a value of $1,500,000. The property was recently sold in a legitimate open marketplace transaction for $1,700,000, subject to a purchase money mortgage of $1,200,000. In assessing the value of the property, the assessor should give the GREATEST weight to the

    A. purchase money mortgage
    B. economic analysis
    C. recent sale price
    D. cost to reproduceless depreciation

4. There are types of expenses incurred by an owner which are usually made an expense of ownership rather than being an expense of the real estate. The one of the following which is an expense of the real estate is

    A. mortgage interest
    B. depreciation on the building
    C. reserves for replacement of short-lived building components
    D. income tax

5. In valuing an old investment type of property, the MOST appropriate method for an assessor to use is

    A. capitalization of income
    B. replacement cost less depreciation
    C. mortgages on the property
    D. gross to net income ratios

6. The sales comparison method which is used in appraising real estate has its basis in in the principle of

    A. contribution   B. change   C. substitution   D. balance

7. The cost approach is the MOST valid approach to use in deriving an assessed value when

   A. construction costs are low
   B. a building is new
   C. the cost of the property is justified by the economic value
   D. the cost of the property is lower than the economic value

8. Which one of the following items is usually excluded when computing the net square feet of an individual apartment in a multi-family building? All

   A. columns whether enclosed or not
   B. ducts and risers
   C. balconies exterior to the apartment
   D. areas within the perimeter walls of the apartment

9. Residential neighborhoods frequently give early warning signs of decline. Which one of the following is LEAST important as an indicator of neighborhood decline?

   A. Change in the nature of the population
   B. Unusual number of "For Sale" signs where permitted
   C. Conversion of large homes into rooming houses
   D. Lack of enforcement of zoning regulations and deed restrictions

10. Marble or stone chips set in Portland cement and polished to a smooth surface is known as

    A. terra cotta
    B. crushed limestone
    C. terrazzo
    D. expanded slag

11. According to the capitalization of income approach to value, if all factors of income, interest rate, and recapture and reversion are the same, the use of a 40-year income projection will bear what relationship to the use of a 10-year income projection?

    A. The use of a 40-year income projection will produce a higher value than the use of a 10-year projection
    B. The decline in gross and net income as the properties become older results in a lower value over 40 years
    C. A 10-year income projection will produce the same value as a 40-year income projection
    D. They would bear no direct relationship to each other since the courts in certiorari cases are abandoning building residual techniques for assessing purposes

12. The one of the following factors which LEAST influences the character of the income stream in the appraisal of income-producing properties is the

    A. amount of income which is expected
    B. certainty of receiving the expected income
    C. timing of the receipt of each component in the expected income stream
    D. reinvestment rate of return on the anticipated net income

13. The capitalization technique used by assessors known as the building residual technique with straight line recapture involves several appraisal assumptions. Which one of the following assumptions is NOT inherent in the use of this technique?

    A. The land value will vary over the economic life of the property
    B. It is necessary for the assessor to predict the remaining economic life of the building
    C. The property value is at its peak at the date the appraisal is made and will continue to decline during the economic life of the property
    D. Income attributable to the building declines year by year over the economic life of the property

14. Assume that you are estimating the replacement costs of a building. Which one of the following would be of GREATEST value to you in making this estimate?

    A. Knowledge of a building's content (cubic capacity)
    B. Zoning floor area ratio (in square feet)
    C. Energy saving devices (in units of energy)
    D. Name of the builder

15. Two homes which are adjacent to each other are identical to each other in every respect, and, therefore, have the same market value of $400,000. Home "A" is assessed $125,000 for land and $400,000 total. Home "B" is assessed $100,000 for land and $400,000 total. The owner of Home "A" files for a reduction of his assessment.
    Of the following, the MOST appropriate response to the request for reduction is that

    A. because of the difference in land value assessments, a reduction will be made in the total assessed value
    B. no reduction is warranted as the total assessed values are the same
    C. the difference in land value assessments is due to the fact that owner "A" has a larger parcel of land
    D. no reduction is warranted because it will disturb the equality of assessment of other similar parcels in the block

16. A main structural element which sustains the joists of a floor is known as a

    A. girder   B. column   C. mullion   D. ridge piece

17. Low ceiling heights in a factory building are a form of depreciation known as

    A. economic obsolescence   B. physical deterioration
    C. accrued depreciation   D. functional obsolescence

18. Crucial to the validity of the principle that reproduction cost, less depreciation, plus land value ordinarily sets an upper limit on value, is the

    A. assumption of little delay in the construction process
    B. accuracy of the cost and depreciation estimate
    C. supply-demand relationship at the time of the appraisal
    D. inclusion of both "hard" and "soft" costs in the cost estimate

19. Suppose that a property with a net income of $100,000 can be purchased for all cash at $1,000,000. If it were to be purchased with $250,000 cash plus a 25-year mortgage at 8% interest in the amount of $750,000 (annual constant 9.37%), the pre-income tax equity rate of return would be, most nearly,

    A. 9.3%   B. 10.5%   C. 11.1%   D. 11.9 %

20. Suppose that an apartment house has an effective gross income of $250,000 and total operating expenses of $150,000. Of the operating expenses, 66 2/3% are considered to be variable and 33 1/3% are considered to be fixed.
If both the effective gross income and the variable expenses increase by 10%, the net operating income will

A. increase by 10%
B. increase by 15%
C. increase by 16 2/3%
D. not increase

21. Suppose that income producing property sells at an indicated overall capitalization rate of 9%.
If the net income ratio for this property is 50%, the gross income multiplier is, most nearly,

A. 4.5
B. 5.5
C. 6.0
D. 6.5

22. A building site of 10,000 square feet located in a C-4-7 zone is worth $500,000. All other things being equal, a zoning change to C-6-7 would make this plot worth

A. $250,000
B. $750,000
C. $1,000,000
D. $600,000

Question 23.

DIRECTIONS: Answer Question 23 on the basis of the following information.

23. Suppose that you are appraising a rent-controlled apartment house which has the following income and expenses as submitted by the owner (you have no reason to question the accuracy of the statement):

Gross Income	$89,030	
Expenses		
Payroll	$7,865	
Fuel	3,680	
Light & Power	2,042	
Painting	4,500	
Plumbing	1,030	
Repairs	4,232	
Supplies	2,785	
Elevator Maintenance	1,314	
Capital Improvements	1,860	
Legal & Audit	900	
Payroll Taxes	450	
Miscellaneous	770	
Mortgage Interest	11,320	
Real Estate Taxes	20,800	
Water & Sewer Tax	862	
Insurance	3,100	
Management	2,700	
Total	$70,210	70,210
Net Income		$18,820

A reconstruction of the above statement for assessing purposes would indicate a net income free and clear of

A. $33,860
B. $32,000
C. $50,000
D. $20,680

Questions 24-25.

DIRECTIONS: Answer Questions 24 and 25 SOLELY on the basis of the information in the paragraph below.

You are reassessing a parcel of property where the land area is 8,273 square feet, zoned C-6-6 and improved with a six-story and basement office building containing a gross area of 45,836 square feet above ground. (The land is currently assessed consistent with the existing zoning.) Seven years after construction of the building, the owners entered into a 75-year net lease with the owner of an adjacent parcel to permit the lessee to utilize the unused development rights inherent in the parcel improved with the six-story office building. The lease called for an annual net rental of $33,000 per annum for the excess development rights.

24. Based on the information in the above paragraph, and disregarding any bonus for plaza, the MAXIMUM number of above-ground development rights that could be transferred is, most nearly,

    A. 37,200 square feet   B.   53,400 square feet
    C. 78,300 square feet   D.   103,500 square feet

25. Based on the information in the above paragraph, the MOST appropriate conclusion regarding the land value of the "granting" parcel is that the

    A. land value should be reduced to conform with the actual use and area of the improvement
    B. land value should remain at its present level because it is assessed in conformity with other parcels on the block which are also zoned C-6-6
    C. land value should be increased because of the net rental being received for the development rights transfer
    D. net-lease rentals should be added to the residual net income of the land, developed by the land residual technique, using the current income and expenses applicable to the six-story office building, and a revaluation of the land should be calculated

KEY (CORRECT ANSWERS)

1.	D	11.	C
2.	A	12.	D
3.	C	13.	A
4.	C	14.	A
5.	A	15.	B
6.	C	16.	A
7.	C	17.	D
8.	C	18.	A
9.	A	19.	D
10.	C	20.	B

21. B
22. B
23. B
24. C
25. D

TEST 2

DIRECTIONS: Each question or incomplete statement is followed by several suggested answers or completions. Select the one that BEST answers the question or completes the statement. PRINT THE LETTER OF THE CORRECT ANSWER IN THE SPACE AT THE RIGHT.

1. In selecting a capitalization rate in today's market there are several factors which must be considered. Some of these factors are reasonably factual while others are judgmental. Of the following factors, which one should be considered PRIMARILY judgmental?

    A. Available ratio of mortgage money to fair market values
    B. The income projection term in years
    C. Interest rate that will attract mortgage money at the time of the appraisal
    D. Maximum full mortgage amortization term available at the time of appraisal

    1.____

2. You are assessing a parcel of land which has been inadequately improved and the net income from the property is insufficient to yield an adequate return on the market value of the land.
   Of the following, the MOST appropriate method of estimating a market value for this parcel of land, assuming redevelopment is 5 years away, is to

    A. appraise the land for its highest and best use and then add a minimal amount for the improvement and adjust this value by a time discount factor
    B. appraise the land for the highest and best use and then deduct the cost of demolishing the improvement and then add the increased value of the land 5 years hence
    C. appraise the property on the basis of its current income and attribute all the value to the land, adjusting the value by taking a 5-year time discount
    D. appraise the land for its highest and best use, then apply a 5-year time discount for the cost of demolition and another 5-year time discount for the resulting land value

    2.____

3. On a street in a district zoned R-2, 40x100 lots have a value of $200,000 and are so assessed based on a front foot value of $5,000. A vacant parcel on this street has a dimension of 60 feet by 100 feet deep. It has been assessed for $300,000 (600 front feet x $5,000). The owner argues that he can only build one house on this plot and, therefore, he should be assessed only for $200,000.
   Of the following, the MOST appropriate response to the owner is:

    A. The 60x100 plot is sufficient for the construction of 2 houses on the plot and hence is more valuable
    B. The owner can build a 2-family house on this size plot and, therefore, it is worth more than a 40x100 plot, and the 2-family house can be easily converted to a 3-family house
    C. The 60x100 plot is worth more than a 40x100 plot although probably not in proportion to their areas, and a modification of the assessed value will be made to reflect a reasonable increment for size
    D. A zoning variance can be obtained which will justify the difference in assessed value

    3.____

19

4. The one of the following statements about the "principle of substitution" which is MOST accurate is that it

   A. is given little weight by the courts
   B. affirms that a builder may depart from building specifications when specified materials are not easily obtainable
   C. has application to the three approaches to value
   D. relates to the alternate choices in selecting the proper approach to value

5. As applied to the appraisal of real property, the *one* of the following statements which is MOST valid about the "principle of anticipation" is that it

   A. provides the basis for the "percentage" clauses in leases
   B. affirms that change is ever present especially with regard to taxes and utility charges
   C. affirms that value is the present worth of future benefits
   D. states that excess profits breed ruinous competition

Questions 6-8.

DIRECTIONS: Answer Questions 6 through 8 on the basis of the information in the following passage.

You are responsible for reviewing, in 2013, the assessment of an office building with 100,000 square feet rentable area. This building rents to several major tenants on 10-year leases and is 100% rented. Based on 2005 figures, the rent is $7.00 per square foot. There are escalation clauses built into the leases for tax increases and operating costs over the 2005 figures. The assessment in 2005 was $3,500,000. The tax rate in 2005 was $60 per thousand assessed, and operating expenses were $1.75 per square foot. The tax rate in 2012 was $87.50 per thousand assessed and operating costs were $2.00 per square foot.

6. Based on the information in the above passage, the tenants' share of the operating costs in 2012 was

   A. 17.5%   B. 50%   C. 25%   D. 12.5%

7. Based on the information in the above passage, the net return to capital in 2012, excluding all operating costs and taxes, was

   A. $821,250   B. $315,000   C. $525,000   D. $725,000

8. Based on the information in the above passage, and assuming you considered a 9% capitalization rate as an appropriate return on capital, how would the rate be reflected in the assessed value in 2013 as opposed to 2005? The assessed value would

   A. *increase,* because gross income is higher
   B. *decrease* to reflect higher operating expenses and taxes
   C. *increase* to offset the tax rate increase
   D. *remain the same*

9. Assume that when you attempt to measure the size of apartments in a recently renovated apartment building, the superintendent of the building denies you access to the premises despite all your efforts.
Of the following, the BEST action to take in this situation is to

   A. call the police and ask them to force entry
   B. enter when the superintendent is not there
   C. call your supervisor to assist you in gaining entry
   D. obtain the measurements from the building plans

10. Assessors and appraisers interview property owners and builders in order to gather data affecting property value. You are *most likely* to encourage those being interviewed to cooperate with you by

    A. limiting the interview only to those areas you wish to discuss
    B. impressing those being interviewed that you are acting as a representative of the government, and, as such, if they fail to cooperate, they are violating the law
    C. explaining procedures and answering questions, when appropriate
    D. letting the person being interviewed initiate the discussion

11. Assume that you are interviewing a veteran for a veteran's exemption under Section 458 of the tax law. You find that he is not qualified to receive an exemption. Of the following, the BEST course of action to take in this situation is to

    A. tell him that he will receive formal written notification of your decision and that you can tell him nothing at present
    B. have your supervisor inform him of the decision not to grant him the exemption
    C. inform him that he is not eligible for the exemption, and if he appeals, his assessment may increase
    D. tell him that he is not eligible for the exemption and explain the reasons why

12. Suppose that you have asked an assistant to gather some data which you need immediately for an important assignment. The assistant tells you that he has a lot of other work to do, and will obtain the information for you when he has the time.
In this situation, the action which would be BEST for you to take first is to

    A. point out that since you are an employee with higher rank, the assistant has to follow your orders
    B. report the assistant's lack of cooperation to your supervisor
    C. ask a more cooperative employee to get the data for you
    D. ask the assistant what work he has to do and why it is needed

13. In carrying out the duties of the job, you may sometimes have to interview people in the field who are uncooperative and even, in extreme cases, verbally abusive. Of the following, the BEST way to *initially* deal with a person who is verbally abusive is to

    A. remain calm and try to find out whether he has a legitimate complaint
    B. end the interview and leave the premises
    C. tell him that you agree with some of his complaints but you have to follow orders
    D. respond in a similar manner until he calms down

14. Suppose that a property owner is reluctant to provide information concerning certain renovations he has made. Of the following, it would be BEST to tell the property owner that

   A. you will send your supervisor to obtain the information
   B. it is important that he give you the information himself, in order for an accurate assessment to be made
   C. if he refuses to provide the information, you will make an overly-high assessment, thus forcing him to reveal the information
   D. the renovations probably will not warrant an increase in his assessment, so he should not be reluctant to give you the information

15. Suppose that while you are in the field, you are approached by a property owner who complains that the amount of the previous year's assessed valuation of his property is higher than that of his neighbor although he claims that there is no difference in the properties. You made both assessments, and have data indicating that the properties are not, in fact, identical.
Of the following, it would be BEST for you to tell this person that

   A. there is a difference in the properties, and explain the basis on which you ascribed his assessment
   B. you cannot discuss the assessment with him; he should file an appeal during the appeal period
   C. if a mistake were made, you will see that it is corrected, but you cannot reveal any information
   D. assessments are based solely on established guidelines; you cannot give him details about his assessment

16. Assume that you are to recommend whether to grant tax exempt status to a non-profit foundation incorporated in the State for the study of Tibetan Buddhist Doctrines, whose charter provides that the corporation is organized solely for the religious purpose of instructing members in the use of Tibetan Buddhism.
Of the following, the MOST important factor in making your recommendation is

   A. your investigations of the actual use of the property to determine that it is being used for its charter purposes
   B. your determination, based on research, whether Tibetan Buddhism is an established religion eligible for tax exempt status
   C. whether or not tax exempt status has been granted to other similar foundations
   D. the number of existing tax exempt properties in your district

17. Assume that you are called upon to assist a senior citizen submit an application for a Senior Citizen exemption on a two-family house he owns. He lives in one apartment and his son lives in the rental apartment. The son pays no rent but pays most of the father's expenses.
The *appropriate* action to take is to

   A. refuse to initiate the application on the ground of ineligibility since the son pays most of the father's expenses
   B. ascribe a rental estimate to the son's apartment, which is then listed as income, and submit the application for determination

C. make a ruling on the applicant's eligibility for the tax exemption based on the percentage of income contributed by the son
D. ascribe a rental estimate to the son's apartment, which is then listed as income, and make a determination on the applicant's eligibility

18. Suppose that a landlord has altered an existing rooming house, converting it to class A apartments.
Under the law, the tax exemption to which he is entitled is:

   A. Full exemption of the increase in building value, exempt for 12 years
   B. Fifty percent of the increase in building value, exempt for 12 years
   C. Full exemption of the increase in building value, decreasing every two years by 20% over a 10-year period
   D. Fifty percent of the increase in building value, decreasing by 5% every year over a 10-year period

18.____

19 Which one of the following is NOT considered taxable real property?

   A. Gas ranges and stoves   B. Safe deposit vaults
   C. Gasoline tanks   D. Window air conditioners

19.____

20. Which of the following items is NOT allowed as eligible funds on which tax exemptions are granted for veterans?

   A. A bonus granted by the State B. G.I interest refund
   C. Refunds on G.I. insurance   D. National Guard drill pay

20.____

KEY (CORRECT ANSWERS)

1. B	11. D
2. D	12. D
3. C	13. A
4. C	14. B
5. C	15. A
6. D	16. A
7. B	17. B
8. D	18. A
9. D	19. D
10. C	20. D

EXAMINATION SECTION
TEST 1

DIRECTIONS: Each question or incomplete statement is followed by several suggested answers or completions. Select the one that BEST answers the question or completes the statement. *PRINT THE LETTER OF THE CORRECT ANSWER IN THE SPACE AT THE RIGHT.*

1. Real property, as legally defined, includes

   A. gas ranges
   B. refrigerators
   C. furniture
   D. heating systems

   1.____

2. Ownership of real estate includes the exclusive right, in every instance, to

   A. take minerals from the sub-surface portions
   B. receive unobstructed light and air from adjacent parcels
   C. use adjacent parcels for access if the property is land-locked
   D. perpetuate a non-conforming use

   2.____

3. The *Bundle of Rights* refers to the

   A. constitutional authority to appropriate property
   B. various rights attached to ownership of real estate
   C. rights of tenants under net lease arrangements
   D. sheaf of papers in a real estate transaction

   3.____

4. Cost equals value when

   A. construction cost indices are stable
   B. national conditions are normal
   C. a new building improves a site most profitably
   D. depreciation is not excessive

   4.____

5. Market value is BEST defined as the

   A. highest price, expressed in dollars, that a property would sell for under the most favorable market conditions
   B. difference between the Cost Approach and Income Approach
   C. average of the three approaches to Value
   D. highest price, expressed in dollars, that a willing, well-informed buyer would pay and a willing, well-informed seller would accept

   5.____

6. In order for an object to have value in an economic sense, it MUST have

   A. an attractive appearance
   B. practical utility
   C. a clear title
   D. tangible materials

   6.____

7. *Highest and Best Use* means

   A. most profitable use
   B. most intensive use
   C. the use which produces the largest dollar income
   D. the largest structure

   7.____

2 (#1)

8. The PROPER point in the appraisal process at which the highest and best use analysis should be made is

   A. correlation of the three approaches
   B. definition of the appraisal problem
   C. final valuation estimate
   D. preliminary survey of the appraisal task

9. The *principle of change* is evidenced in

   A. restrictive covenants running with the land
   B. the evolutionary stages in the life of a neighborhood
   C. the land residual technique
   D. the Sheridan-Karkow formula

10. The *principle of balance* is exhibited in the

    A. process of making adjustments in a market data analysis
    B. refining of the capitalization rate through the utilization of quality considerations on a relative basis
    C. agents in production in a property existing in such relative proportions that they produce the maximum residual net income to land
    D. number of apartments and rooms in an apartment house

11. The *principle of contribution states* that

    A. all three approaches to value contribute equally to the final valuation estimate
    B. land and buildings contribute to the creation of economic rents
    C. the value of an agent in production depends upon how much it adds to net income
    D. only business enterprise makes a real contribution

12. In the cost approach to value, under ideal conditions, land value is estimated by the

    A. analysis of market data on a comparative basis
    B. analysis of local tax assessment records
    C. land residual technique
    D. property residual technique

13. In estimating Replacement Cost, the majority of appraisers use the

    A. quantity survey method
    B. unit cost in place method
    C. ENGINEERING NEWS RECORD
    D. unit cost per cubic or square foot method

14. In the Cost Approach of an appraisal of a parcel of real property, the Replacement Cost estimate should include cost of

    A. wall-to-wall carpeting
    B. insurance during construction of improvements
    C. agent's management fees
    D. washing machines

15. *Accrued Depreciation* is BEST defined as the

    A. provision for recapture of capital invested in improvements on the land
    B. measures taken to guard against excessive decay and physical deterioration
    C. difference between the cost of replacement, new, and the present appraised market value
    D. loss in value resulting from any and all causes

16. In estimating accrued depreciation, it is considered the BEST practice to use

    A. the *observed condition* technique
    B. Age-Life tables
    C. Bureau of Internal Revenue tables
    D. Real Estate Board statistics

17. Only one of the three major components of accrued depreciation is said to result from causes extrinsic to the property being appraised.
    This component is

    A. curable functional obsolescence
    B. physical deterioration
    C. economic obsolescence
    D. incurable functional obsolescence

18. The test to determine whether an item of functional obsolescence is curable or incurable is

    A. the consensus of opinion among real estate brokers
    B. the expenditure required to cure it, an item requiring an expenditure of more than $100,000 being incurable
    C. whether the cost of effecting the cure can be recouped in equivalent or greater value
    D. whether the item is mechanical or structural, the former being curable, the latter incurable

19. A cause of economic obsolescence is

    A. utilization of sub-standard specifications in construction of improvements under appraisal
    B. inadequate electric wiring
    C. poor architectural planning for improvements under appraisal
    D. rent control legislation

20. For purposes of capitalization, net income is USUALLY computed before the expense of

    A. debt service charges   B. property taxes
    C. replacement reserve   D. management

21. Capitalization may be described as

    A. establishing the income to be received
    B. converting the net income into value
    C. computing the amortization on the investment
    D. taking an interest and depreciation return on the building value

22. The estimate of economic life is based PRIMARILY on the _____ of the improvement.

    A. physical durability
    B. age
    C. size
    D. relative competitive utility

23. Net income imputable to land is capitalized in perpetuity because

    A. the entire investment is amortized out of the building income
    B. the land returns are presumed to last forever since urban land does not physically depreciate and land may thus be successively utilized
    C. investors capitalize land income in this manner since they cannot take depreciation on the land for tax purposes
    D. land represents a reversionary interest

24. The capitalization process must provide for recovery of the building investment over the economic life of the building because

    A. the investment should be recovered at the same approximate rate as the building is anticipated to decline in value from depreciation
    B. it is customary to recover every asset out of income, regardless of whether it is depreciable or not
    C. the investor always believes the amortization on the mortgage is designed to achieve the recovery of his capital for him
    D. amortization may not be equal to depreciation

25. The capitalization process referred to as *direct capitalization plus straight line depreciation* is based on an assumption that the

    A. income stream will remain level
    B. building has suffered a substantial amount of functional obsolescence
    C. income stream will decline over the years
    D. curing of most accrued depreciation is possible

26. In capitalization techniques, the method of providing for future depreciation that generally permits highest valuation is the

    A. annuity system   B. quantity survey
    C. sinking fund   D. straight line method

27. The building residual technique is applicable when

    A. accurate building cost data is available
    B. the building improves the site to its highest and best use
    C. land is in short supply in the market
    D. there is an abundance of market data relating to comparable sites

28. A capitalization rate is the

    A. amount of taxes levied upon a capital gain
    B. equalization rate for property taxes
    C. rate of return necessary to attract capital
    D. rate of capital depreciation

29. The *Band of Investment* method of selecting a capitalization rate is

   A. built up on the *safe rate*
   B. applicable only when land residual technique will be used
   C. based on analysis of sales
   D. based on weighted average of mortgage and equity rates

30. Since the use of the Inwood (annuity) factor provides for complete depreciation of a real estate investment over its assumed economic life, the use of such technique in the appraisal of improved real property necessitates

   A. provision for substantial tax levies
   B. an estimate of the value of the land reversion
   C. an especially careful neighborhood analysis
   D. a very thorough inspection of improvements

31. In the land residual technique, the appraiser

   A. bases his opinion on careful analysis of market data
   B. need not inspect the building unless there are building violations on it
   C. sometimes bases his estimates on a hypothetical structure representing highest and best use
   D. is concerned only with raw land costs

32. The so-called *overall* capitalization rate is BEST arrived at by

   A. obtaining the ratio of net income to selling price of comparable properties
   B. consulting the Dow Service for the standard capitalization rates most frequently used
   C. examination of Census Statistics
   D. employing the summation or *build-up* technique

33. In real estate appraisal work, the market data approach should particularly be used

   A. when the sales market has experienced substantial activity
   B. when cost information is too difficult to obtain
   C. when the subject property is new
   D. only when a residential property is being appraised

34. The market data approach is used for direct valuation of properties and it is also useful in

   A. making quantity surveys
   B. making insurance appraisals
   C. establishing capitalization rates
   D. controlling depreciation

35. The heart of the market data approach is

   A. thorough checking of deed registration
   B. careful averaging of sales statistics
   C. thorough-going analysis of the records of the Building Department
   D. careful comparisons between comparables and property being appraised

KEY (CORRECT ANSWERS)

1.	D		16.	A
2.	A		17.	C
3.	B		18.	C
4.	C		19.	D
5.	D		20.	A
6.	B		21.	B
7.	A		22.	D
8.	D		23.	B
9.	B		24.	A
10.	C		25.	C
11.	C		26.	A
12.	A		27.	D
13.	D		28.	C
14.	B		29.	D
15.	C		30.	B

31. C
32. A
33. A
34. C
35. D

TEST 2

DIRECTIONS: Each question or incomplete statement is followed by several suggested answers or completions. Select the one that BEST answers the question or completes the statement. *PRINT THE LETTER OF THE CORRECT ANSWER IN THE SPACE AT THE RIGHT.*

1. Appraisals for any purpose in the real estate field, in an economic sense, are required because 1.____

    A. a high unit cost is involved
    B. realty is a non-standardized commodity
    C. it is a customary practice
    D. brokers are usually uninformed

2. The legal basis for the estimation of full value in real estate tax assessment appraisals is 2.____

    A. stabilized market value, without regard to cyclical extremes
    B. a combination of the market comparison and income approaches
    C. cost for improvements, less any depreciation, plus land value estimated by comparison
    D. capitalized value of the residual net income

3. In a purely objective sense, no matter what the purpose of the appraisal may be, the market value of the real estate at a given moment is ALWAYS 3.____

    A. identical
    B. varied
    C. mixed
    D. dependent on the approach

4. Certiorari appraisals are unique in technique because 4.____

    A. they frequently result in court actions
    B. the tax rate is incorporated in the capitalization rate
    C. all three value approaches are used
    D. they are used in no other state except New York

5. There is an effective limitation on the height of reinforced concrete structures because 5.____

    A. the large columns required take up too much floor space and impair floor layouts
    B. the structural framework is too rigid for climatic changes
    C. the building code limits the height of reinforced concrete structures
    D. it is expensive to haul concrete to excessive heights

6. Aside from zoning restrictions, the height of a steel skeleton frame building is limited by the 6.____

    A. cost of the steel framing
    B. labor cost involved at great heights resulting from labor scarcity
    C. cost of utility installations
    D. adequacy of the net rent received on the construction cost of the last floor

7. A typical semi-fireproof apartment house has 7.____

    A. all wood floors but masonry walls
    B. concrete first floor arch, wood upper floors, load bearing masonry walls
    C. light steel bar joists, 2" poured concrete floors, load bearing masonry walls
    D. all concrete floors and load bearing masonry walls

8. Continual flaking of paint on the inner surface of an outer masonry wall PROBABLY indicates

   A. a poor paint job caused by adulterating the paint with a chemical
   B. shoddy construction permissible under an inadequate building code
   C. driving rains from the east
   D. a need for pointing up the loose and dislodged mortar in the joints

9. The appraiser makes an inspection of the realty under appraisal because

   A. it keeps him informed on building construction
   B. he must be an engineer to be qualified
   C. the results of the inspection have a direct bearing on the value
   D. a very detailed description of the realty is expected of him

10. The LEAST costly heating system to install and service, which takes the least amount of space and costs the most for fuel, is

    A. coal stoker
    B. oil burner
    C. gas-fired hot water
    D. utility steam

11. The type of material used for plumbing risers, branches, and crotons has a direct bearing on value because

    A. the better the quality and the more durable the material, the higher the anticipated net income
    B. superintendents are prohibited by union rules from making repairs to the plumbing system
    C. the mechanical equipment depreciates in the same manner as the building shell
    D. some types of material become functionally obsolete faster than others

12. An inspection of the rentable space is as important as an inspection of the building shell and equipment because

    A. the appraiser can determine if there are any furnished units
    B. it establishes the basis for a comparable rent analysis
    C. the occupancy must be checked against the leases
    D. it makes the report look more impressive

13. Which one of the following is GENERALLY found in an unaltered old law tenement?

    A. Combination washtub and bathtub
    B. Dumbwaiters
    C. Central heat
    D. Off-foyer layouts

14. Which one of the following is MOST generally found in a new law tenement?

    A. A standpipe system
    B. Dumbwaiters
    C. Colored tile baths
    D. Windowless rooms

15. If an inspection revealed that an apartment house was dangerously underwired, the appraiser should PRIMARILY solve this in his appraisal report by

    A. advising the owner to correct the condition forthwith
    B. advising the client to notify the Building Department immediately
    C. subtracting the capital cost of re-wiring from the market value, after reflecting the rent increases permitted by the Rent Commission in the net income
    D. ignoring the condition on the assumption that the owner will eventually replace the wiring

16. If a building is of competitive, that is, average construction quality, and if it has been well maintained to the date of the appraisal, the LEAST significant type of depreciation is probably

    A. super session
    B. physical deterioration
    C. functional obsolescence
    D. inadequacy

17. The type of air conditioning system installed in most new apartment houses is

    A. air-cooled central system with adequate ducts
    B. peripheral system circulating chilled water
    C. heavy duty fan system
    D. unit in wall sleeve

18. Land use is usually the MOST intensive in _____ districts.

    A. apartment   B. hotel   C. loft   D. office

19. A significant decline in employment in a city may affect real estate market values through

    A. economic obsolescence
    B. neighborhood decay
    C. removal of middle class to the suburbs
    D. the aging process

20. The removal of some of the middle income class from the core of the city to the suburbs has resulted in a(n)

    A. increase in the available supply of dwelling units
    B. decline in controlled rents
    C. acceleration of physical deterioration and economic obsolescence in those central residential neighborhoods
    D. opportunity to modernize controlled rent apartments

21. Downtown major retail sections have been adversely affected PRIMARILY by

    A. obsolete buildings
    B. too many taxicabs and too few buses
    C. poor planning of merchant associations
    D. outlying shopping center competition

22. If published material were not available, the BEST source for obtaining the net annual addition to the housing stock would be

    A. condemnation records

B. tax and assessment records
C. the Register's Office
D. building and demolition permits

23. The trend referred to as *decentralization* is caused LARGELY by

A. encroachment of industry into residential areas in outlying cities throughout the country
B. rent control legislation
C. removal of commerce, industry, and people from the heart of the city to outlying cities or to the periphery
D. inequitable tax assessment policies

24. The cubical content of an office building was 2,100,000 cubic feet. The Dow Service Valuation Calculator gave $1.10 as the net field reproduction cost. The appraiser added 20% to cover all miscellaneous costs and excavation. Depreciation was estimated at 2 1/2% per annum. The building was 25 years old on the appraisal date. Land value was estimated at $15,000 a front foot for the 200' x 100' plot.
The total value by the cost approach is MOST NEARLY

A. $4,039,500
B. $4,762,000
C. $5,191,300
D. $6,244,000

25. The quantity survey method of cost estimation is not used by most market value appraisers because

A. appraisal groups oppose it
B. they are not qualified to use it
C. cost has no importance in valuation
D. the unit-in-place method is better

26. An over-calculation or over-estimation of building cost, assuming a particular level of rent is obtainable, will

A. influence lenders on the mortgage to require less amortization
B. penalize the land value by the approximate amount of the over-calculation of the building cost
C. result in a faulty depreciation allowance for income tax purposes
D. make necessary the engagement of a cost expert on a sub-contract basis

27. The construction cost of a six-story semi-fireproof apartment house is less than that of a fireproof reinforced concrete apartment house of similar size by APPROXIMATELY

A. 40%   B. 30%   C. 15%   D. 10%

28. The cost approach can ALWAYS be used in any appraisal because

A. it can be used as a ceiling of possible market value for the real estate
B. no appraisal can be made without it
C. the physical components of realty are the primary bases for market value
D. it makes the appraisal report more convincing as a result of the cost figures

29. The assessor was assigned to re-appraise for property tax purposes a 60-year-old loft-type structure that was 50% vacant. Many similar structures in the same district had been demolished, and the plots improved with new commercial buildings.
Under the circumstances, which appraisal approach, of the following, would BEST be utilized?

   A. Reproduction cost, less depreciation, plus land value
   B. Replacement cost, plus land value
   C. Market comparison, treating the improvement as almost fully depreciated
   D. the building residual method of capitalization

30. The assessor was assigned to re-appraise for property tax purposes a privately-owned, specially designed and constructed art gallery with high ceilings and ornate construction, for which there was no market in its present use. He concluded that it would not be practical to convert the structure to another use should the art gallery use terminate. He decided to use the cost approach and worked out a reproduction cost for the structure.
In the absence of a market for similar structures, the depreciation computation should MOST probably be based on

   A. May's quantity survey method of computing depreciation
   B. a sinking fund technique
   C. an age-life method based on a straight-line depreciation allowance
   D. an observation derived from personal experience

31. In comparing the results of the cost approach and the income approach when assessing a new building on a given plot, the assessor noted that the income approach yielded a greater total value, despite the use of a high capitalization rate.
Assuming the assessor's cost calculations to be accurate, the differential can BEST be attributed to the fact that

   A. there is always a higher total value when the income approach is used rather than the cost approach
   B. there is usually an increment in value attributable to the land over its acquisition cost, underlying a successfully rented and completed building in a market of equilibrium
   C. the cost approach never reflects the value obtained from the income approach because the former is independent of the rents obtained in the property
   D. the law does not permit equipment in the realty to be treated as real fixtures subject to real estate taxation

32. The assessor was asked to estimate the market land value underlying a one-story store building. The property had recently sold for $1,200,000. The land assessment was $400,000, and the total assessment was $800,000.
Using the assessment ratio extraction process, the assessor should estimate the land value at

   A. $300,000   B. $500,000   C. $600,000   D. $800,000

33. The assessor's unit lot value for a typical side street had been established at $500,000. A vacant corner plot 100' x 75' on the same street sold for $3,000,000. The Hoffman-Neill rule depth factor for 75 feet was 84.49. Assuming standard corner and key lot increments, the unit lot value indicated by the sale is MOST NEARLY

   A. $625,000   B. $700,000   C. $800,000   D. $890,000

34. One of the BEST means of finding the appropriate overall capitalization rate for income property on a market comparison basis is the

    A. earnings price ratio of similar properties
    B. long-term government bond rate in the money market
    C. risk rates in the market
    D. mortgage interest rates

35. You are asked to assess a six-story apartment house on a 100' x 100' plot. You find records of four sales of similar properties.
Which one has no applicability?

    A. R.S. $.55 mortgage $125,000
    B. R.S. $77. mortgage $80,000 P.M.M. $30,000
    C. R.S. $110. mortgage $65,000
    D. Stated consideration: $1,800,000

KEY (CORRECT ANSWERS)

1.	B	16.	B
2.	C	17.	A
3.	A	18.	D
4.	B	19.	A
5.	A	20.	C
6.	D	21.	D
7.	B	22.	B
8.	D	23.	C
9.	C	24.	A
10.	C	25.	B
11.	A	26.	B
12.	B	27.	C
13.	A	28.	A
14.	B	29.	C
15.	C	30.	C

31. B
32. C
33. B
34. A
35. A

TEST 3

DIRECTIONS: Each question or incomplete statement is followed several suggested answers or completions. Select one that BEST answers the question or completes the statement. *PRINT THE LETTER OF THE CORRECT ANSWER IN THE SPACE AT THE RIGHT.*

1. Which one of the following is an INCORRECT technique for analyzing comparable sales?

    A. Ratio of selling price to assessed valuation
    B. Applying locational differential rating factor
    C. Selling price per unit of measurement
    D. Going back fifteen years in checking sales

    1.____

2. The appraiser employed in a certiorari proceeding submitted twenty-five sales, eighteen of which were made prior to the appraisal date, three within six months after the appraisal date, and the balance two and one-half years after the appraisal date.
The MAXIMUM number of sales which the trial justice could admit as evidence of value was

    A. 23   B. 21   C. 19   D. 17

    2.____

3. The market comparison approach is frequently considered the primary or best approach, provided the

    A. income approach is used as a check
    B. subject property is a standardized type and recent comparable market sales are numerous
    C. reproduction cost, less age-life depreciation, plus land value, yields the same result
    D. appraiser subscribes to a sales service

    3.____

4. The assessor was appraising a newly completed apartment house which, in his judgement, was worth less than its replacement cost because of some serious deficiencies in design, layout, and equipment.
In capitalizing the net income, the CORRECT capitalization method to apply to this new building is the _____ method.

    A. building residual   B. land residual
    C. property residual   D. land reversion

    4.____

5. You wish to establish a capitalization rate for the capitalization of net income, before any deduction for depreciation. You decide the Band of Investment Theory is best for this purpose. Debt service charges for similar property is running 8% on a 60% mortgage. Equity returns currently are 10%.
The MOST appropriate capitalization rate is

    A. 7.60%   B. 8.80%   C. 8.90%   D. 9.10%

    5.____

6. Of the following, the BEST mathematical means of capitalizing a net rental from property occupied by an AAA-1 tenant under a thirty year net lease is

    A. annuity table, as Inwood's Premise
    B. interest plus sinking fund
    C. interest plus straight-line depreciation
    D. interest rate, after subtracting depreciation

    6.____

7. The land residual method of capitalization must be used with great caution, particularly when the building has not yet been constructed, because

   A. it requires exceptional technical competence
   B. the leverage factor can produce gross distortions in the residual land return
   C. construction costs are difficult to estimate
   D. it is unethical to capitalize income attributable to a building not yet constructed

8. The method of capitalization which recognizes the valuation principle that land value should never be penalized or discounted merely because of the inadequacy of a depreciated structure is the _____ method.

   A. gross multiplier
   B. net multiplier
   C. building residual
   D. Kniskern-Schmutz

9. Land value under a rent-controlled apartment house was estimated by comparison at $1,000,000. Net income after all expenses except debt service charges was $120,000. The building's economic life was estimated at 25 years and the interest rate at 6%. The annuity factor for 25 years at 6% was 12.78.
   The total value of land and improvements was

   A. $1,766,800
   B. $1,873,600
   C. $2,056,530
   D. $2,593,600

10. The equity return was $4,000. Debt service charges were $6,000. The property sold for $150,000.
    The overall rate of return, free of mortgage debt, was MOST NEARLY

    A. 5.8%   B. 6.2%   C. 6.7%   D. 7.5%

11. The assessor was asked to appraise, for property tax purposes by the property residual method, a department store property under a 40-year lease at $1,000,000 a year. Building life and the lease term are considered coincident. Land value at lease expiration was estimated at $10,000,000. The annuity factor for 40 years at 7% interest was 13.3. The deferment factor for 40 years at 7% interest was .07.
    The present value is MOST NEARLY

    A. $9,800,000
    B. $12,500,000
    C. $13,300,000
    D. $14,000,000

12. A new retail shopping center was considered to represent the highest utilization of the site. It produced a total net income of $1,000,000. The building cost was $8,000,000. Economic life was 40 years. Interest rate was 7%. Assuming straight-line depreciation and employing the most appropriate capitalization methods, the total value is MOST NEARLY

    A. $32,650,000
    B. $26,300,000
    C. $21,250,000
    D. $11,430,000

13. For the property in the preceding question, the ratio of land to total appraised value is MOST NEARLY

    A. 20%   B. 30%   C. 40%   D. 50%

14. You are appraising a vacant lot 25' x 75', 25' from the corner. 14.____
    Which of the following would you consider in estimating the size of the unit lot?

    A. Corner influence, plus Hoffman-Neill factor
    B. Corner and key influence
    C. Key influence, plus Hoffman-Neill factor
    D. Key influence

15. The RECORD AND GUIDE reported the following sale: Park Ave., 908-910 (5:149-37 15.____
    swc, 80th (Nos. 70-76) 81.2 x 80.6, 14 sty. apt; Harry and Jane Fischel Foundation
    (Albert Wald, v.pres.) 960 Park Ave. to 910 Park Ave., Inc. 910 Park Ave.; B&S; 1st mtg.
    $165,734.19; PM mtge. $489,151.08; Apr. 30; May 2 '57; A $235,000. $470,000 (RS
    $725.45).
    What is the selling price and cash payment, respectively?

    A. $825,234.19; $170,348.12
    B. $1,413,583.72; $569,250.00
    C. $319,681.41; $320,281.00
    D. $975,432.00; $251,684.44

16. Using the sales figures given in the preceding question and assuming the depth factor for 16.____
    80' is 87.73, the number of unit lots and the unit lot value, respectively, are MOST
    NEARLY _____ unit lots and _____.

    A. 3.27; $78,904.00   B. 3.69; $91,283.00
    C. 3.92; $69,524.00   D. 3.72; $111,130.00

17. According to the Tax Department, the assessor's field book must contain 17.____

    A. notations on national real estate conditions for each tax year
    B. annuity tables pasted on the inside fold
    C. the actual condition of all buildings in course of construction as of taxable status
       date
    D. the telephone numbers of taxpayers

18. The CHIEF function of the Tax Department's Research Bureau is to 18.____

    A. engage in primary research in real estate, economics, and valuation techniques
    B. prepare research reports for the City Planning Commission
    C. tabulate the ratio of selling prices to assessed values in various cities throughout
       the country
    D. act as an adjunct of the Certiorari Bureau

19. The property cards furnished each assessor do NOT contain 19.____

    A. sales and leases
    B. court decisions
    C. construction costs
    D. national real estate market index

20. Which one of the following is NOT entitled to partial or complete tax exemption? 20.____

    A. Medical society   B. Parsonages
    C. Trade association   D. Veterans' organization

21. In New York City, exempt property is MOST NEARLY what percent of the total of all property? 21.____

    A. 15%   B. 25%   C. 30%   D. 35%

22. The *Assessor's Report for Certiorari Hearing,* in addition to providing a detailed physical description, also computes 22.____

    A. the capitalization of the income
    B. the percent of net on the assessed value
    C. the operating costs per cubic foot
    D. a quantity survey cost estimate

23. An example of a typical expense usually listed under Item 9, OTHER EXPENSES, in an Application for Correction of Assessed Valuation of Real Estate is 23.____

    A. hall and corridor painting
    B. plumbing repairs
    C. liability insurance
    D. management fees

24. In connection with an Application for Additional Veteran Exemption, the item of information which the assessor must obtain is the 24.____

    A. cost of capital improvements to property since purchase
    B. quantity survey cost estimates from reliable contractors
    C. type of veteran's discharge
    D. date on which the veteran purchased the property

25. A remission of real estate from taxation occasionally occurs when 25.____

    A. a corporation has a foreign charter
    B. taxes have been in arrears for three or more years
    C. an *in rem* proceeding is pending
    D. a corporation qualifies for tax exemption

KEY (CORRECT ANSWERS)

1.	D		11.	D
2.	B		12.	D
3.	B		13.	B
4.	A		14.	C
5.	B		15.	A
6.	A		16.	D
7.	B		17.	C
8.	C		18.	A
9.	A		19.	D
10.	C		20.	C

21. C
22. B
23. D
24. A
25. D

EXAMINATION SECTION
TEST 1

DIRECTIONS: Each question or incomplete statement is followed by several suggested answers or completions. Select the one that BEST answers the question or completes the statement. *PRINT THE LETTER OF THE CORRECT ANSWER IN THE SPACE AT THE RIGHT.*

1. Deed restrictions imposed by sellers of real property are very effective devices for maintaining the character of real estate developments and for protecting property values. A restriction which has been OUTLAWED by recent Supreme Court decisions is that which

    A. controls the architectural style of improvements since the court believed this would result in stereotyped neighborhoods and prevent modern styles from emerging
    B. limits lands and other site improvements such as fences, washlines, and TV antennae since owners of properties not having such restriction enjoy these benefits
    C. is contrary to the public interest or is based on race, creed, or color
    D. defines the size and qualities of buildings to be constructed since this prevents an owner from improving his property to its highest and best use

    1.____

2. Transferrability is a legal concept which has an effect on the determination of property value. In order to have value, property must be transferrable.
    The concept of transferrability necessarily implies all of the following EXCEPT

    A. control of the use of the property
    B. physical mobility of the property
    C. ownership
    D. control of the right to give the property away

    2.____

3. Equality and uniformity of assessment requires that all types of properties be assessed at the relative values of one type to the other and that all individual properties be valued relatively one to the other. Assume that the relationship of assessment to full value is 50%.
    Which one of the following is overassessed in terms of equality and uniformity?

    A. A home with a full value of $500,000 is assessed for $150,000.
    B. A vacant lot whose full value is $200,000 is assessed at $100,000.
    C. A warehouse whose full value is $1,000,000 is assessed at $600,000.
    D. An office building with a full value of $10,000,000 is assessed at $4,000,000.

    3.____

4. Property subject to taxation under State statutes is termed real estate, real property, or, in some instances, simply land. Included is the land itself, all buildings, articles, and structures erected upon the land or affixed to the land.
    In assessing a bowling alley for real property tax purposes, which of the following should NOT be assessed? The

    A. land on which the bowling alley is situated
    B. foundation, walls, and roof of the building
    C. central air conditioning system which cools the building
    D. actual bowling alleys which are removable

    4.____

5. Listed below are three statements relating to characteristics of the real estate market:
   I. The real estate market in the United States lacks centralized governmental control
   II. Bid and price offerings of buyer and seller are NOT generally publicized
   III. Real estate parcels are not standardized in respect to size or shape

   Of the three statements presented above, the ones which represent ACCURATE statements about the real estate market are

   A. I, II, III
   B. I and II, but not III
   C. II and III, but not I
   D. none of the above

6. A property owner is dissatisfied with his assessment and his application for correction is denied by the Tax Commission and tri-board hearings.
   The one of the following which is the CORRECT procedure for the property owner to follow is to

   A. petition the Commissioner of the City Department of Real Estate to overrule the decision
   B. request the state real estate board to review the assessing authorities' decision
   C. initiate legal proceedings within the provisions of the state and local statutes
   D. apply for a hearing before the City Planning Commission

7. One of the tests that distinguishes trade fixtures from real property is the

   A. size of the item in question
   B. value of the item
   C. manner in which the item is installed
   D. estimated useful life of the item

8. The *present worth of future benefits arising out of ownership* is known as

   A. value
   B. capital asset
   C. annuity
   D. increment

9. The borrower of a mortgage loan is primarily liable for the payment of the mortgage debt and signs a pledge as the promise to pay.
   In the event that there are several borrowers, the term which should be used to describe their obligation is

   A. jointly
   B. severally
   C. jointly and severally
   D. in common

10. As a characteristic of value, scarcity is a relative term.
    In determining the value of land, scarcity must be considered in relation to all of the following EXCEPT

    A. demand
    B. supply
    C. possible alternate uses of the land
    D. economic encumbrances of developers and investors

11. Of the following, the statement MOST likely to be considered accurate about building cost estimates is that such estimates

    A. should not vary, as the exact price of materials and labor can be determined at any given date
    B. are not subject to wide variations since a building is merely the combination of materials and labor brought together in accordance with specifications
    C. can vary considerably because of the nature of the contracting business and the fluctuations in labor and materials costs at different times and places
    D. are extremely accurate as builders are able to use cost services that are developed from experience, surveys, and statistical evidence

11.____

12. In a realty investment, there are various charges which absorb the gross income produced by the investment. The gross income itself represents a percentage of the value of the investment. Assume that mortgage charges, owner's equity interest, real estate taxes, and operating expenses absorb the gross income completely and that the gross income represents 18.18 percent of value.
The gross income multiplier that could be used to arrive at the value is

    A. 5.5 B. 6.0 C. 6.5 D. 7.0

12.____

13. One method of estimating reproduction cost is unit-in-place analysis.
If, under this method, it is determined that the cost of one square foot of a brick wall is $37.50, the TOTAL cost of the four walls of a one-story, 18-foot-high building containing 4,000 square feet, built on the front 2/3 of a 40 x 150 foot lot is

    A. $94,500 B. $189,000 C. $270,000 D. $540,000

13.____

14. A religious organization is entitled to a real property tax exemption where such organization is non-profit, organized for its exempt purpose, and used exclusively for such exempt purpose.
Which one of the following properties owned by a religious organization most probably would NOT be exempt from taxation? A

    A. building housing a religious school
    B. playground adjacent to a religious school
    C. parking lot used by a religious school
    D. building leased by a religious school to a caterer

14.____

15. A veteran's exemption assumes that a veteran has received certain funds related to his military service used in the purchase or improvement of his home. Assume that John Doe owns a home on Smith Street in which he has used all of his eligible funds and has received a $2,000 veteran's exemption. He decides to sell this home and purchase a larger home on Jones Street.
Which one of the following actions by John Doe would MOST likely enable him to transfer his $2,000 veteran's exemption to his new home on Jones Street?

    A. He buys the home on Jones Street while waiting for a purchaser for his Smith Street home.
    B. He rents his home on Smith Street and purchases the home on Jones Street.
    C. He purchases the home on Jones Street, and then on the very next day he sells his home on Smith Street.
    D. He first sells his home on Smith Street and then the very next day purchases the home on Jones Street.

15.____

16. Assume that an assessor is capitalizing the net income of a parcel of property for assessment purposes.
Of the following, the information of LEAST concern to the assessor would be that the

   A. fire insurance on the building indicated a value far exceeding the value produced by capitalizing the income
   B. actual rent was considerably lower than rent being paid for similar properties
   C. lessee of the property contracted to pay all increases in taxes above a certain base period
   D. lessee had an option to buy at a certain fixed price

17. Land has physical and economic characteristics.
The physical characteristics of land which has caused it to be classified as real estate is its

   A. availability for different uses
   B. return on investment
   C. use as collateral in securing loans
   D. immobility

18. In considering comparable sales as a method of valuing property for assessment purposes, two main factors arise. One is the distance between the site being assessed and the comparable property. The other is the recency of the comparable sale.
Which one of the following sales is most likely to be considered unreasonable for use as a comparable sale? In valuing

   A. a golf course, the only golf course sale available was made five years ago, and the course was located 50 miles away
   B. an industrial building, a similar building in the same industrial park sold two years ago is used as a comparable sale
   C. an office building, the recent sale of a large store located immediately adjacent to the office building is used as in comparable sale
   D. a one family home, the recent sale of an identical home situated in a similar community two miles away is considered a comparable sale

19. The taxpayer has the burden of proving that the assessed value on his property is excessive. The valuation established by the assessor is presumed correct. However, the presumption of correctness disappears in the face of contradictory evidence.
Of the following, the LEAST convincing evidence provided by the taxpayer to support his contention of an excessive assessment is that

   A. in a recent sale of comparable property, the sales price was lower than his assessment
   B. twenty years ago, he purchased the subject property at a price considerably lower than the assessment
   C. the replacement costs of subject property less depreciation produce a value less than the assessment
   D. the capitalization of the net income of the property produces a value considerably less than the assessment

20. A real property tax assessment case is being heard by the court. Which one of the following statements represents pertinent evidence for the court to consider in rendering its decision? The

    A. full value of the property in question
    B. owner's inability to pay the real property taxes
    C. local assessor's lack of sufficient experience to render a just decision
    D. doubling of real property taxes on this property over the last ten years

21. The principle that value at a given location is proportionate to street frontage receives added import at corner lots. The highest lot values in business areas will almost always be the corner lots.
    This statement MOST accurately defines the term

    A. corner influence   B. increment
    C. intangible asset   D. key influence

22. That use of the land which will provide the greatest net return to the land over a reasonable period of time is a definition of the term

    A. reversion   B. valuation
    C. highest and best use   D. capitalization

23. An agreement whereby the owner of a property holds it off the market in return for a consideration is called a(n)

    A. sales agreement   B. binder
    C. escrow   D. option

24. The upright side of a doorway, window, or fireplace is called the

    A. buttress   B. apron   C. jamb   D. cantilever

25. An ornamental railing or parapet made of coping or a hand rail and balusters is called a(n)

    A. kerf   B. balustrade   C. batten   D. ashlar

26. A hinged window frame, commonly made so the window will open outward is called a

    A. casement   B. double-hung   C. bay   D. sash

27. *Purchasing power, utility,* and *supply* are terms generally associated with

    A. value   B. cost   C. price   D. capital

28. In most real estate transactions, a buyer finances the major portion of the purchase price by borrowing and pledging to assure the repayment of the purchase loan with interest over a specific period of time.
    The one of the following which does NOT represent a method of financing commonly used in the purchase of realty is a

    A. mortgage   B. promissory note
    C. bond   D. stock option

29. Assume that, as an assessor, you are busily working in your office when you are interrupted by a telephone call. The caller requests information which you do not have. The PROPER action for you to take is to tell the caller

   A. you are sorry but you don't have that information
   B. that you would like to help him, but you are just too busy
   C. to hold on while you find out who can give him the correct information, and then transfer his call.
   D. what you guess might be the correct answer to his question

30. Assume that you are an assessor. A property owner comes into your office to check the assessment on his property. In the course of the discussion, he becomes angry and abusive.
   Of the following, the MOST effective action you can take is to

   A. tell the person that you will not tolerate that kind of behavior and will have him removed from the office if he doesn't stop
   B. display your irritation at his behavior so that he will know he has not intimidated you
   C. call the building security office immediately
   D. keep your self-control and try to calm the person

31. Assume that you are an assessor. You receive a phone call in the office from an agitated property owner. The information you give him is not what he had hoped to hear, and he asks you to give him your name.
   Of the following, the MOST appropriate action for you to take is to

   A. give the property owner your name
   B. ask your supervisor to speak to the caller
   C. tell him that you are not required to give your name
   D. find out why he wants to know your name

32. Following are four steps that should be taken to solve a problem involving public relations:
   I. Weigh and decide; consider possible actions
   II. Follow-up; check the results of your actions
   III. Get the facts; determine the exact nature of the problem
   IV. Take action; implement your plan
   Which of the following choices shows the PROPER sequence of the above steps an assessor should take?

   A. IV, II, III, I
   B. III, I, IV, II
   C. I, IV, II, III
   D. II, III, IV, I

33. As an assessor, you may be required to answer letters from the public.
   Which of the following techniques SHOULD be used in such correspondence?

   A. Try to make the public feel grateful to your agency for the services it receives from the agency.
   B. Do not volunteer information other than that requested.
   C. Be as clear as possible, but avoid verbosity.
   D. Try to use as much technical language as possible to impress the public with your knowledge.

34. In which section of his appraisal report would an appraiser include detailed maps, floor plans, and blue prints?

   A. Introduction
   B. Analysis and conclusions
   C. Appendix
   D. Preface

35. The one of the following items which would NOT generally be included in the *Summary of Important Conclusions* section of an appraisal report is

   A. net income expectancy
   B. the estimate of land value and highest and best use
   C. capitalized value estimate
   D. population trends

36. In addition to the basic information contained in an appraisal report, certain auxiliary documents must accompany a complete narrative report.
   The one of the following NOT required to be included in this report is

   A. a letter of transmittal relating to the narrative report
   B. a statement of qualifications of the appraiser
   C. disclosure of the appraiser's personal finances and business interests unrelated to the specific property
   D. the certificate of the appraiser

37. Public recording of instruments relating to property rights is used to notify third parties of the existence of rights in property and to establish the priority of rights or claims to property.
   Since some instruments merge with a subsequently executed instrument, the one instrument which is very SELDOM publicly recorded is the

   A. ownership deed
   B. mortgage
   C. mechanic's lien
   D. contract of sale

38. Zoning is the device by which planning is expressed in concrete terms and consists of ordinances and maps defining the geographic areas within which various types of land use limitations are enforced.
   In light of this definition,

   A. zoning is limited to the geographic area over which the municipal authorities have jurisdiction and may not be extended beyond those limits
   B. zoning generates city growth and insures the development of a particular land use in a given area
   C. an area zoned for commercial use will insure the success of any such use in that area
   D. zoning controls automatically coincide with those uses dictated by market trends

39. The demand for single family homes is a composite of price, income, and subjective interests or desires in which investments in homes are determined in some degree by attempts to benefit from speculation in a rising market. This anticipation of rising markets serves to intensify increased real estate activity. Conversely, these same subjective elements which serve to reinforce a rising market may disappear in a declining market and so hasten the decrease in real estate investments.
This statement indicates that

    A. home ownership is so dependent on family whims that price is not a determinant of the decision to purchase a house
    B. there is a direct relationship between business conditions and the rates of increase and decrease in the demand for single family homes
    C. home purchasing activity remains on a constant level because of the compelling desires of most families to own their own home
    D. most families are so possessed of the desire to have a home of their own that demand offsets any other factors against purchase

40. A borrower obtained an $80,000 mortgage loan under the level-or-constant payment plan for 20 years at 7 percent interest. His monthly payments amount to $775.30. Which of the following represent the CORRECT amounts for interest and for payment on principal for each of the first two monthly payments?

A.	1st month	Interest	$560.00	Principal	$215.30
	2nd month	Interest	$558.50	Principal	$216.80
B.	1st month	Interest	$466.70	Principal	$308.60
	2nd month	Interest	$464.90	Principal	$310.40
C.	1st month	Interest	$672.00	Principal	$103.30
	2nd month	Interest	$671.10	Principal	$104.20
D.	1st month	Interest	$466.70	Principal	$308.60
	2nd month	Interest	$433.10	Principal	$342.20

KEY (CORRECT ANSWERS)

1.	C	11.	C	21.	A	31.	A
2.	B	12.	A	22.	C	32.	B
3.	C	13.	B	23.	D	33.	C
4.	D	14.	D	24.	C	34.	C
5.	A	15.	D	25.	B	35.	D
6.	C	16.	A	26.	A	36.	C
7.	C	17.	D	27.	D	37.	D
8.	A	18.	C	28.	D	38.	A
9.	C	19.	B	29.	C	39.	B
10.	D	20.	A	30.	D	40.	B

TEST 2

DIRECTIONS: Each question or incomplete statement is followed by several suggested answers or completions. Select the one that BEST answers the question or completes the statement. *PRINT THE LETTER OF THE CORRECT ANSWER IN THE SPACE AT THE RIGHT.*

Questions 1-3.

DIRECTIONS: Answer Questions 1 through 3 according to the information given in the following passage.

Section 502 of the State Real Property Tax Law – Form of Assessment Roll – states in Subdivision 2 that when a tax map has been approved by the State Board, reference to the lot, block and section number or other identification numbers of any parcel on such map should be deemed as sufficient description of such parcel. Otherwise, the name of the owner, last known or abutting owners and a description sufficient to identify the parcel must be listed.

Subdivision 3 states that the assessment roll shall contain a column for the entry for the assessed value of land exclusive of improvements for each separately assessed parcel followed by a column for the entry of the total assessed valuation. It then states that only the total assessed valuation shall be subject to judidical review.

1. A city in the state has a tax map describing real property by section, block and lot, and this map has been approved by the state board. Robert Roberts purchased a one-family home from William Williams at 777 Seventh Street, Woodside, described as Section 22, Block 222, Lot 2 on the tax map.
According to the above passage, which description on the Assessment Roll is legally INCORRECT?

   A. William Williams, 333 Third Street, Woodside, Section 22, Block 222, Lot 2
   B. Robert Roberts, 777 Seventh Street, Woodside, Section 22, Block 222, Lot 2
   C. William Williams, 777 Seventh Street, Woodside, Section 22, Block 222, Lot 2
   D. Robert Roberts, 777 Seventh Street, Woodside, Section 22, Block 222, Lot 3

1.____

2. An assessing district in the city has a tax map describing real property by section, block and lot. This map has not as yet been approved by the state board.
According to the passage, which one of the following descriptions would NOT be correct?

   A. Amos Jones, 999 Smith Boulevard, Elmhurst
   B. Section 37, Block 750, Lot 9
   C. Property located at 999 Smith Boulevard, Elmhurst, surrounded by properties owned by John Doe, Richard Roe, Sam Samuels, and Alvin Abrams
   D. Property on Smith Boulevard, Elmhurst, bounded on the East by John Doe, on the West by Richard Roe, on the South by Sam Samuels, and on the North by Alvin Abrams

2.____

3. According to the passage, which of the following entries of assessed valuations would be PROPER under the provisions of Subdivision 3?

   A. Land - $500,000; Total - $1,000,000
   B. Improvement - $500,000; Total - $1,000,000
   C. Total - $1,000,000; Improvement plus land - $1,000,000
   D. Land - $500,000; Improvement - $500,000

Questions 4-6.

DIRECTIONS: In each of Questions 4 through 6, four sentences are given. For each question, choose as your answer the group of numbers that would represent the MOST logical order of these sentences if they were arranged in paragraph form.

4. I. However, a photograph or a map of a city at a given moment of time fails to show the dynamic character of the city's growth.
    II. Thus, if the location of a certain type of area has changed from one period to another, it is possible to determine the direction and speed with which such movements have occurred by using devices of this kind.
    III. One method for collecting the necessary information is by the use of time interval maps.
    IV. Several photographs taken at different time intervals or several maps for different periods reveal the processes of change.

    A. I, IV, II, III
    B. III, I, II, IV
    C. III, I, IV, II
    D. I, III, IV, II

5. I. In small towns, all neighborhoods may be within easy walking distance of schools, shopping centers, places of employment, and amusement parks.
    II. Adequacy of transportation, like so many other factors involved in neighborhood analysis, is a relative matter.
    III. In most larger cities, however, transportation has a vital bearing on neighborhood stability since neighborhoods which do not have access to desirable transportation facilities at reasonable cost suffer from the competition of those which are more favorably located.
    IV. In such cases, transportation is of no significance in determining neighborhood stability.

    A. II, I, IV, III
    B. III, I, II, IV
    C. III, IV, I, II
    D. II, IV, III, I

6. I. If he plans to sell lots, he needs to know something of the demand for lots of the type and price range he is considering.
    II. In addition, the subdivider or developer needs information about the potential market for the specific types of products which he intends to sell.
    III. Prior to undertaking a new land development project, it is essential that the general conditions of the market be understood.
    IV. If he intends to subdivide and completely develop a tract of land, constructing homes, apartments, a shopping center, or other buildings on the lots, he will need information about their salability or rentability.

    A. IV, III, I, II
    B. III, II, I, IV
    C. I, III, II, IV
    D. I, II, IV, III

Questions 7-10.

DIRECTIONS: Answer Questions 7 through 10 according to the information given in the following passage.

In capitalizing the net income of property to produce a value, certain expenses are permitted to be deducted from gross income. Even though the premises may be fully rented, it is proper to deduct from the gross income an allowance for vacancy. All expenses attributable to the maintenance and upkeep of the premises are deductible. These include heat, light and power, water and sewers, wages or employees and expenses attributable to wages, insurance, repairs, and maintenance, supplies and materials, legal and accounting fees, telephone, rental commission, advertising, and so forth. If the premises are furnished, a reserve for the depreciation of personal property is deductible. A capital improvement to the building is not a deductible expense. Real estate taxes should not be deducted as an expense. Instead, taxes should be factored as part of the overall capitalization rate.

It is proper to allow an expense for management of the building even in cases where the owner himself is manager. But, payments of interest and principal of the mortgage are not a properly deductible expense. Real property is appraised free and clear of all encumbrances. Otherwise, two identical buildings located next to each other might be valued differently because one has a greater mortgage than the other.

7. According to the above passage, the one of the following which is NOT a proper deductible expense during the year in which the expense is incurred is the cost for

    A. advertising to rent the premises
    B. accounting fees
    C. utilities
    D. putting in central air conditioning

8. According to the above passage, the one of the following statements concerning deductible expenses which is CORRECT is that

    A. a vacancy allowance is a proper deductible expense even though the premises may be fully rented
    B. real estate taxes are a proper deductible expense
    C. if the owner manages his own property, he cannot charge a management fee as a deductible expense
    D. payments for interest and principal of the mortgage are proper deductible expenses

9. According to the passage, two identical adjacent buildings CANNOT receive different valuations because of differences in their

    A. mortgages   B. net income
    C. leases   D. management fees

10. According to the passage, an owner of furnished premises may set aside a reserve as a deductible expense for all of the following EXCEPT

    A. refrigerators   B. carpeting
    C. bookcases   D. walls

Questions 11-13.

DIRECTIONS: Answer Questions 11 through 13 according to the information given in the following passage.

The standard for assessment in the State is contained in Section 306 of the Real Property Tax Law. It states that all real property in each assessing unit shall be assessed at the full value thereof. However, the Courts of the State have not required assessors to assess at 100% of full value. Assessments of property for real estate tax purposes at less than full value are not invalid if they are made at a uniform percentage of full value throughout the assessing district. In assessing real property, full value is equivalent to market value.

In determining market value of real property for tax purposes, every element which can reasonably affect value of property ought to be considered, and the main considerations should be given to actual sales of the subject or similar property, cost to produce or reproduce the property, capitalization of income therefrom, and the combination of these factors.

11. According to the above passage, the one of the following statements which is INCORRECT is that all real property in each assessing unit

    A. must be assessed at full value
    B. shall be assessed at full value or at a uniform percentage of full value
    C. may be assessed at 50% of full value
    D. may be assessed at 100% of full value

12. According to the above passage, the one of the following elements of value which should be given the LEAST consideration in determining market value is

    A. actual or comparable sales
    B. reproduction cost
    C. amount of mortgage
    D. capitalization of income

13. According to the passage, the basis for the legality of assessing units making assessments at a uniform percentage of full value rather than at full value is

    A. Section 306 of the Real Property Tax Law
    B. decisions of the State Courts
    C. judgments of individual assessors
    D. decisions of municipal executives

Questions 14-17.

DIRECTIONS: Answer Questions 14 through 17 according to the information given in the following passage.

Depreciation – Any reduction from the upper limit of value. An effect caused by deterioration and/or obsolescence. Deterioration is evidenced by wear and tear, decay, dry rot, cracks, encrustations, or structural defects. Obsolescence is divisible into two parts, functional, or economic. Functional obsolescence may be due to poor planning, mechanical inadequacy or overadequacy, functional inadequacy or overadequacy due to size, style, or age. It is evidenced by conditions within the property. Economic obsolescence is caused by changes external to the property, such as neighborhood infiltrations of inharmonious groups or property uses, legislation, etc. It is also the actual decline in market value of the improvement to land from the time of purchase to the time of sale.

14. According to the above passage, a form of physical deterioration can be caused by 14._____

    A. termite infestation
    B. zoning regulations
    C. inadequate wiring
    D. extra high ceilings

15. According to the passage, a form of economic obsolescence may be caused by 15._____

    A. structural defects
    B. poor architectural design
    C. changes in zoning regulations
    D. chemical reactions

16. According to the passage, the statement which BEST explains the meaning of depreciation is that it is a loss in value 16._____

    A. caused only by economic obsolescence
    B. resulting from any cause
    C. caused only by wear and tear
    D. resulting from conditions of changes external to the property

17. According to the passage, the lack of air conditioning in warm climates is 17._____

    A. a form of physical deterioration
    B. a form of functional obsolescence
    C. a form of economic obsolescence
    D. not a form of depreciation

Questions 18-21.

DIRECTIONS: Answer Questions 18 through 21 according to the information given in the following passage.

In determining the valuation of income producing property, the capitalisation of income is accepted as a proper approach to value. Income producing property is bought and sold for the purpose of making money. How much an investor would pay would, of course, depend on how much he could earn on his investment. The amount he would earn on his investment is called a return. The amount of return depends on the degree of risk involved.

If one has $1,000,000 to invest, it can be put in a bank account at perhaps a 5 percent return. In the bank, the money is relatively safe so the return is lower. If the money were invested by purchasing a block of stores in a depressed area, of course, one would not be satisfied with a 5 percent return. This is what the capitalization of income comes down to — the better the return, the higher the risk. This is the approach an experienced real estate investor uses in determining what he would pay for property.

18. According to the above passage, which one of the following investments would an experienced real estate investor with $1,000,000 MOST likely choose? A(n)

   A. apartment building in a slum area yielding a 6 percent return
   B. office building rented to professionals yielding a 6 percent return
   C. shopping center in a depressed area yielding a 10 percent return
   D. warehouse rented on a long-term lease to a major corporation yielding a 10 percent return

19. According to the passage, in the capitalization of income, the relationship between the degree of risk and the rate of return GENERALLY is expected to be

   A. indeterminate   B. variable   C. inverse   D. direct

20. According to the passage, in purchasing income producing property, the one of the following which would NOT be a factor influencing an experienced real estate investor is the

   A. socio-economic characteristics of the area in which the property is located
   B. rate of return on investment
   C. original cost of the property
   D. degree of risk involved

21. According to the above passage, the property listed below which would be LEAST likely to be valued by the capitalization of income is a(n)

   A. apartment house with no vacancies
   B. office building rented to 70 percent of capacity
   C. shopping center with several new tenants
   D. vacant lot located next to a factory

Questions 22-25.

DIRECTIONS: Answer Questions 22 through 25 according to the information contained in the following passage.

The cost approach is used by assessors mainly in valuing one family homes and properties of a special nature which are not commonly bought and sold and do not produce an income.

There are three aspects to the cost approach to valuation. The first is the actual cost of construction. Where the property has recently been built, the cost of constructing the property is relevant. It, however, may not be a true test as to its value. The building may have been constructed so as to serve the special needs of the owner. What it costs to construct may not truly reflect its value; it may be worth more or less. If it is income producing property, the income may be more or less than expected. It may be sold for more or less than it cost to build.

The second aspect is replacement cost and applies to older structures. It involves the construction of a similar type of building with the same purpose. It does not require the use of the same materials or design.

Reproduction cost is the third aspect, and it also applies to older structures. It involves construction with the exact same materials and design. The cost in the two latter aspects is construction at today's prices with an allowance made for depreciation from the day the original building was constructed.

22. According to the above passage, which one of the following is a CORRECT statement concerning the cost approach to valuation? 22._____

   A. In determining value by the replacement and reproduction cost methods, an allowance must be made for depreciation from the day the building was originally constructed.
   B. The cost approach method is the best method to apply in valuing an office building.
   C. When a structure has been recently built, its actual cost is the best method of determining its value.
   D. The fact that a structure has been built to meet the special needs of the occupant is a relevant factor in valuation.

23. An assessor, in valuing a ten-year-old apartment house, finds that its original construction cost was $12,000,000. In capitalizing its net income, he realizes a valuation of $8,000,000. In using the replacement cost method and allowing for depreciation, the assessor arrives at a valuation of $9,000,000. 23._____
   According to the above passage, which one of the following valuations is LEAST acceptable for this apartment house?

   A. $12,000,000   B. $8,000,000   C. $9,000,000   D. $8,500,000

24. The construction cost of a recently built structure is relevant to value, but may not be a true test of value. According to the passage, which one of the following statements CORRECTLY explains why this is true? 24._____

   A. The builder may not know how to construct economically.
   B. A building can depreciate very quickly.
   C. The building may have been built to satisfy certain unique specifications.
   D. Cost-of-construction is not an accepted method of valuation.

25. According to the passage, which one of the following statements CORRECTLY defines the essential difference between the replacement cost and reproduction cost aspects of the cost approach? 25._____

   A. Replacement cost is used only in assessing older buildings; reproduction cost is used only when the building has been recently constructed.
   B. Reproduction cost does not include any allowance for depreciation; replacement cost allows for depreciation from the date of construction of the original building.
   C. Replacement cost involves construction with the same exact materials; reproduction cost does not require the use of the same materials.
   D. Reproduction cost involves construction with the exact same materials and design; replacement cost does not require the use of the same materials and design.

Questions 26-31.

DIRECTIONS: Answer Questions 26 through 31 on the basis of the information given in the following passage.

Realty, because of fixity in investment, immobility in location, and necessity for shelter purposes, lends itself readily to economic controls when such are deemed essential to serve social or political ends, or where the interest of health, safety, and morality of community pop-

ulation or the nation at large warrants it. Realty has consistently been recognized as a form of private property which is sufficiently invested with public interest to warrant its control either under the police power of a sovereign state and its branches of government or by direct and statutory legislation enacted within the framework of the governmental constitution.

Whenever war or catastrophe causes a sudden shifting of population or suspension of building operations, or both, an imbalance is brought about in the supply and demand for housing. This imbalance in housing demand and supply creates conditions of insecurity and instability among the tenants who fear indiscriminate eviction or unwarranted upward rental adjustments. It is this background of possible exploitation during times of economic stress and strain that underlies the enactment of emergency rent control legislation.

Although rent control has been in effect in many communities, particularly the larger metropolitan communities, since the end of World War II, the attitude of all levels of government is to view this form of legislation as temporary and to hasten, as far as their power permits, a return to normal relations between landlords and tenants.

26. According to the passage, the reason that realty can conveniently be subjected to controls is due to

    A. public interest
    B. site immobility
    C. population shifts
    D. moral considerations

27. The above passage includes as a justification for the imposition of economic controls all of the following EXCEPT

    A. threats to physical safety
    B. socio-politico considerations
    C. dangers to health in the community
    D. requirements of police powers

28. According to the passage, a LIKELY cause for a cessation of construction might be a

    A. natural disaster
    B. change in the demand for housing
    C. change in the supply of housing
    D. demographic fluctuation

29. According to the passage, of the following, a tenant's insecurity would MOST likely result in his fear of

    A. reduction in necessary services
    B. loss in equity
    C. rent increases
    D. condemnation proceedings

30. According to the passage, indiscriminate evictions by landlords during periods of economic difficulties constitute

    A. unlawful acts
    B. justifiable measures
    C. desirable actions
    D. exploitation of tenants

31. According to the above passage, economic controls of realty have been in effect on a widespread basis since

   A. 1918   B. 1945   C. 1953   D. 1964

Questions 32-35.

DIRECTIONS: Answer Questions 32 through 35 on the basis of the following passage.

Although zoning is a phase of city planning and is concerned with land use control of private property, zoning powers are better known and more generally applied than most city planning powers. Zoning powers predate the formulation of a master plan and even the formation of the planning commission itself. The widespread application of zoning powers is evident from a survey conducted by the International City Managers' Association. As reported in the Municipal Yearbook, 98 percent of all cities in excess of ten thousand population had enacted comprehensive zoning ordinances governing the utilization of privately owned land. Since 60 percent of all urban land is generally held under private ownership, the impact of zoning laws upon income and value of real property is most significant.

32. Of the following, the one whose land use is MOST likely to be affected by zoning controls, according to the passage, is

   A. Gimbel's Department Store
   B. the Port Authority terminal
   C. the New York Public Library at 42nd Street
   D. the Federal Building

33. According to the passage, in relation to the powers of city planning, zoning powers are

   A. not as familiar to the general public
   B. formulated subsequent to the establishment of the powers of the planning commission
   C. more general in their application
   D. likely to develop as a result of the community's master plan

34. According to the passage, if there are 200 cities in the United States with a population exceeding 10,000 persons, the number of such cities LIKELY to have enacted comprehensive zoning laws is

   A. 190   B. 192   C. 194   D. 196

35. According to the passage, for each 400 acres of urban land, it is LIKELY that the amount of land which would be privately owned would be _____ acres.

   A. 220   B. 240   C. 260   D. 280

KEY (CORRECT ANSWERS)

1.	D		16.	B
2.	B		17.	B
3.	A		18.	D
4.	C		19.	D
5.	A		20.	C
6.	B		21.	D
7.	D		22.	A
8.	A		23.	A
9.	A		24.	C
10.	D		25.	D
11.	A		26.	B
12.	C		27.	D
13.	B		28.	A
14.	A		29.	C
15.	C		30.	D

31.	B
32.	A
33.	C
34.	D
35.	B

TEST 3

DIRECTIONS: Each question or incomplete statement is followed by several suggested answers or completions. Select the one that BEST answers the question or completes the statement. *PRINT THE LETTER OF THE CORRECT ANSWER IN THE SPACE AT THE RIGHT.*

1. A property decreases in value from $450,000 to $350,000. The percent of decrease is MOST NEARLY
    A. 20.5%   B. 22.2%   C. 25.0%   D. 28.6%

2. The fraction $\frac{487}{101326}$, expressed as a decimal, is MOST NEARLY
    A. .0482   B. .00481   C. .0049   D. .00392

3. The reciprocal of the sum of 2/3 and 1/6 can be expressed as
    A. 0.83   B. 1.20   C. 1.25   D. 1.50

4. Total land and building costs for a new commercial property equal $250.00 per square foot.
   If the investors expect a 10 percent return on their costs, and if total operating expenses average 5 percent of total costs, annual gross rentals per square foot must be AT LEAST
    A. $37.50   B. $42.50   C. $50.00   D. $60.00

5. The formula for computing the amount of annual deposit in a compound interest-bearing account to provide a lump sum at the end of a period of years is $X = \frac{r}{(1+r)^{n-1}}$ (X is the amount of annual deposit, r is the rate of interest, and n is the number of years). Using the formula, the annual amount of the deposit at the end of each year to accumulate to $200,000 at the end of 3 years with interest at 2 percent on annual balances is
    A. $61,200.00   B. $62,033.30   C. $65,359.00   D. $66,666.60

6. An investor sold two properties at $1,500,000 each. On one, he made a 25 percent profit. On the other, he suffered a 25 percent loss.
   The NET result of his sales was
    A. neither a gain nor a loss
    B. a $200,000 loss
    C. a $750,000 gain
    D. a $750,000 loss

7. A contractor decides to install a chain fence covering the perimeter of a parcel 75 feet wide and 112 feet in depth. Which one of the following represents the number of feet to be covered? _____ feet.
    A. 187   B. 364   C. 374   D. 8,400

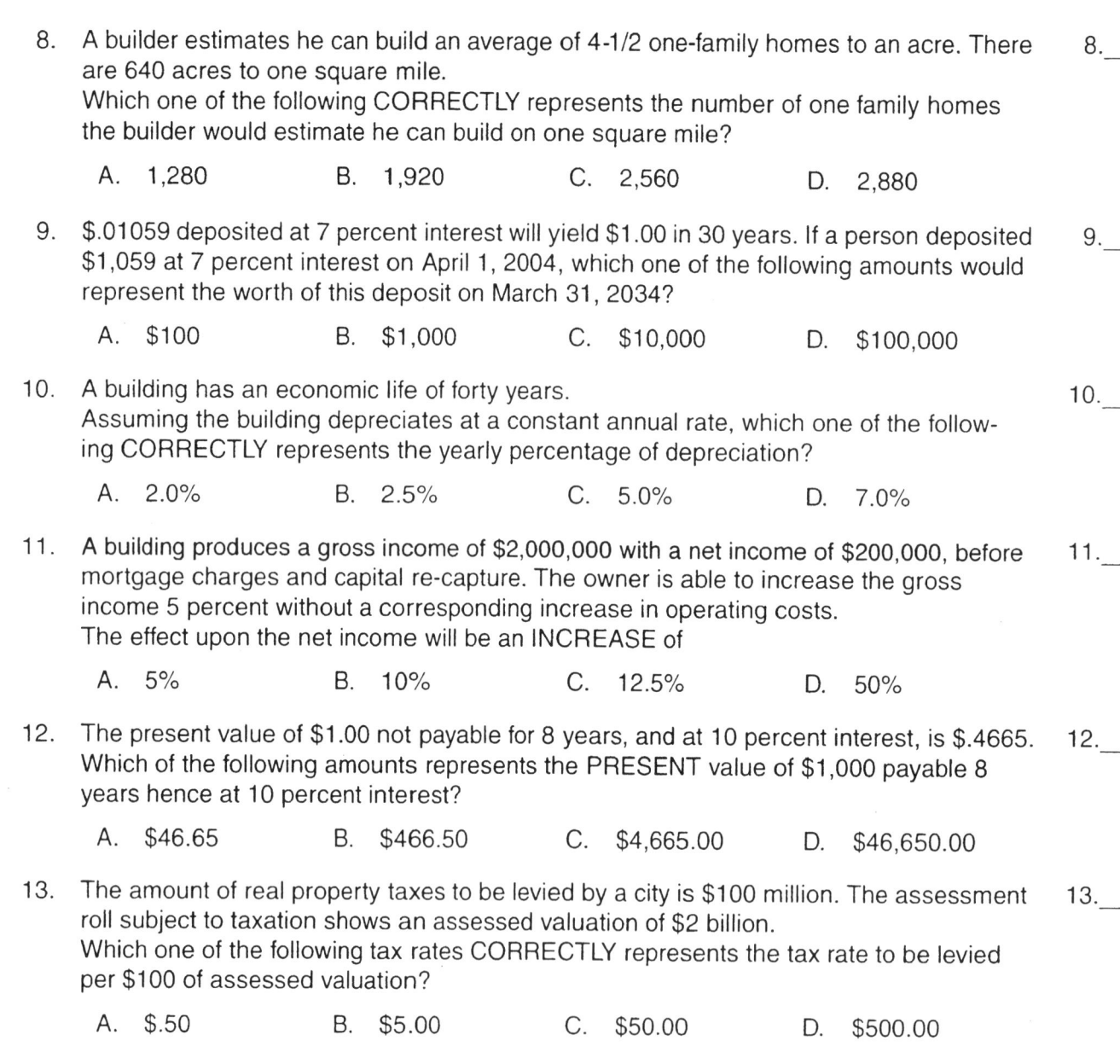

8. A builder estimates he can build an average of 4-1/2 one-family homes to an acre. There are 640 acres to one square mile.
   Which one of the following CORRECTLY represents the number of one family homes the builder would estimate he can build on one square mile?

   A. 1,280   B. 1,920   C. 2,560   D. 2,880

9. $.01059 deposited at 7 percent interest will yield $1.00 in 30 years. If a person deposited $1,059 at 7 percent interest on April 1, 2004, which one of the following amounts would represent the worth of this deposit on March 31, 2034?

   A. $100   B. $1,000   C. $10,000   D. $100,000

10. A building has an economic life of forty years.
    Assuming the building depreciates at a constant annual rate, which one of the following CORRECTLY represents the yearly percentage of depreciation?

    A. 2.0%   B. 2.5%   C. 5.0%   D. 7.0%

11. A building produces a gross income of $2,000,000 with a net income of $200,000, before mortgage charges and capital re-capture. The owner is able to increase the gross income 5 percent without a corresponding increase in operating costs.
    The effect upon the net income will be an INCREASE of

    A. 5%   B. 10%   C. 12.5%   D. 50%

12. The present value of $1.00 not payable for 8 years, and at 10 percent interest, is $.4665.
    Which of the following amounts represents the PRESENT value of $1,000 payable 8 years hence at 10 percent interest?

    A. $46.65   B. $466.50   C. $4,665.00   D. $46,650.00

13. The amount of real property taxes to be levied by a city is $100 million. The assessment roll subject to taxation shows an assessed valuation of $2 billion.
    Which one of the following tax rates CORRECTLY represents the tax rate to be levied per $100 of assessed valuation?

    A. $.50   B. $5.00   C. $50.00   D. $500.00

Questions 14-19.

DIRECTIONS: The graph below presents data on two demographic characteristics and the rate of new home construction in Empire State during the period 1995 through 2006. Answer Questions 14 through 19 on the basis of the graph alone.

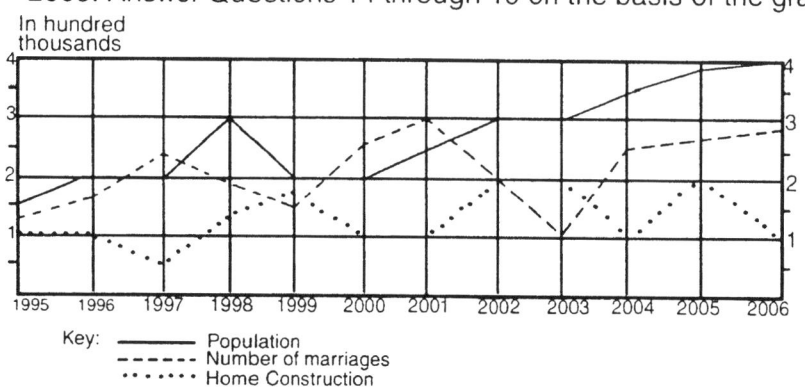

Key: ——— Population
     ----- Number of marriages
     ••••• Home Construction

14. The increase in population in Empire State from 2000 to 2003 was approximately 14.____

    A. 50,000   B. 100,000   C. 150,000   D. 200,000

15. The year with the greatest increase in population was 15.____

    A. 1998   B. 1999   C. 2002   D. 2004

16. The greatest overall increase in the number of marriages occurred during the period 16.____

    A. 1997-1999   B. 1998-2000   C. 2000-2002   D. 2004-2006

17. In the period from 1995 through 2002, the trend in home construction could BEST be described as 17.____

    A. increasing steadily throughout the period
    B. remaining relatively stable
    C. overall increasing with periods of decline
    D. overall decreasing with fluctuations

18. If the rate of population increase that occurred between 1997 and 1998 occurs between 2006 and 2007, the population of Empire State in 2007 would be 18.____

    A. 400,000   B. 500,000   C. 600,000   D. 800,000

19. The period when there was no change in the number of homes constructed and no change in population was 19.____

    A. 1996-1997   B. 1999-2000   C. 2000-2001   D. 2002-2003

Questions 20-25.

DIRECTIONS: The graph below presents data on the rate of new office construction in the uptown, midtown, and downtown areas of Gotham City for the period from 1987 through 2001. Answer Questions 20 through 25 on the basis of the information provided in the graph.

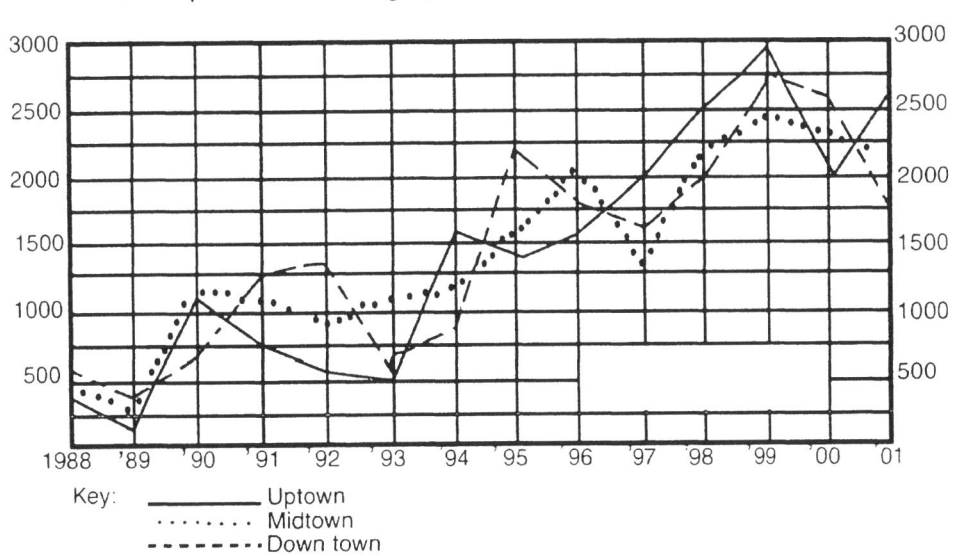

Key: ———— Uptown
      .... Midtown
      -------- Down town

4 (#3)

20. The amount of office space which was constructed in Gotham City in the year 1997 is MOST NEARLY _____ square feet. 20.____

    A. 2,100,000   B. 3,500,000   C. 4,900,000   D. 5,700,000

21. In which of the following years was the LEAST amount of office space constructed in the downtown area? 21.____

    A. 1988   B. 1991   C. 1993   D. 1995

22. The year with the GREATEST amount of new office construction was 22.____

    A. 1990   B. 1994   C. 1999   D. 2001

23. In the years 1995 through 1999, the overall trend in new uptown office space construction could BEST be described as 23.____

    A. generally stable
    B. steadily increasing with small annual fluctuations
    C. generally increasing with large annual fluctuations
    D. steadily decreasing with major annual fluctuations

24. The GREATEST increase in percentage of new office space construction occurred in the year 24.____

    A. 1998   B. 1995   C. 1992   D. 1990

25. Consider the relationship between the amount of midtown office construction in 1990 and 1994. 25.____
If the same relationship would exist in 2001 and 2005, the amount of midtown office construction in 2005 would be _____ square feet.

    A. 1,300,000   B. 1,600,000   C. G. 2,100,000   D. 2,500,000

KEY (CORRECT ANSWERS)

1. B   11. D
2. B   12. B
3. B   13. B
4. A   14. B
5. C   15. A

6. B   16. B
7. C   17. C
8. D   18. C
9. D   19. D
10. B   20. C

21. A
22. C
23. B
24. D
25. C

EXAMINATION SECTION
TEST 1

DIRECTIONS: Each question or incomplete statement is followed by several suggested answers or completions. Select the one that BEST answers the question or completes the statement. *PRINT THE LETTER OF THE CORRECT ANSWER IN THE SPACE AT THE RIGHT.*

1. When using the cost depreciation approach, value equals

    A. the reconciled value of comparables
    B. income divided by the capitalization rate
    C. vacant land value plus depreciated building value
    D. gross income times the standard multiplier

2. Which of the following is CORRECT concerning appraisers?

    A. An appraiser's license is necessary
    B. They are compensated on a fee basis according to the difficulty of their assignment
    C. They search for market price
    D. All of the above

3. When the question of title arises, the broker should

    A. be sure to base any statement he makes upon his opinion only
    B. do nothing since brokers have no duty to the prospect because there is no fiduciary relationship
    C. advise the prospect to procure an abstract to be examined by a competent attorney or obtain title insurance
    D. tell the prospect to seek the seller's opinion

4. A broker may have a branch office

    A. near his main office
    B. anywhere in the country
    C. in his home
    D. all of the above

5. A broker has fiduciary duties because he

    A. is licensed
    B. adheres to a code of ethics
    C. is responsible to his principal
    D. is bound by contract

6. A broker has a listing for $10,000.00. He obtains an offer of $12,000.00. The broker buys the property for $10,000.00 and resells it for $12,000.00.
   This is a(n)

    A. conspiracy
    B. overage
    C. illegal commission
    D. lawful practice

7. A salesperson can have an escrow account

    A. in the normal course of business
    B. only with the approval of his employer

C. only with the approval of his employer and the licensing commission
D. under no circumstances

8. Which of the following statements BEST describes the relationship between the broker and his prospect?

   A. They are dealing at arm's length.
   B. The broker must report any facts or rumors concerning the property.
   C. They are governed by the rule *caveat emptor.*
   D. The prospect can rely upon material statements.

9. A salesperson selling his own property

   A. must have the broker place the ad and need not state that he is a registered salesperson
   B. can advertise in his own name and need not state that he is a registered salesperson
   C. can avoid the rule about advertising in the broker's name and advertise as for sale by owner, indicating that he is a registered salesperson and giving his employer's telephone number
   D. must have the broker place the ad and give the broker's and salesperson's names

10. If a broker wishes to obtain a true option, he must

    A. pay a definite, valuable consideration
    B. divest himself of his identity as a broker
    C. pay a definite valuable consideration and divest himself of his identity as a broker
    D. do no more than any other purchaser

11. Which of the following is(are) CORRECT?
    I. A contract for sale of a homestead requires two witnesses.
    II. An individual must file annually for homestead exemption.
    The CORRECT answer is:

    A. I *only*
    B. II *only*
    C. Both I and II
    D. Neither I nor II

12. Eminent domain is thought of in connection with

    A. courts
    B. the government
    C. private enterprise
    D. death intestate with no heirs

13. An encumbrance affects

    A. existing mortgages
    B. title
    C. possession
    D. zoning

14. The secret sale of more than one-half of a business's assets is prevented by the

    A. Fictitious Names Act
    B. State Real Estate License Law
    C. Division of State Land Sales
    D. Bulk Sales Act

15. Which of the following are proof of merchantable title? 15.____

    A. Abstract and survey
    B. Abstract and title insurance
    C. Title insurance and survey
    D. None of the above

16. Which of the following is(are) CORRECT? 16.____
    A(n)
    I. abstract is an assurance of clear title
    II. title search required for closing always takes place on the day of closing; therefore, the buyer is protected when he receives the deed

    The CORRECT answer is:

    A. I *only*
    B. II *only*
    C. Both I and II
    D. Neither I nor II

17. The mortgage insurance premium for the insurance on FHA 203(b) loans is 17.____

    A. one-half of 1 percent of the remaining principal balance payable monthly
    B. paid with the annual casualty insurance premium
    C. one-half of 1 percent of the monthly payment
    D. paid with the discount at the closing

18. The PRIMARY concern of any real estate investment should be 18.____

    A. tax shelter aspects
    B. depreciation deductions
    C. economic soundness
    D. location

19. Which of the following are INCORRECT concerning mortgages? 19.____

    A. Signed by the mortgagee
    B. Signed by two witnesses
    C. Signed by the mortgagor
    D. Both A and B

20. Broker Brown receives three offers on a parcel of property he has listed. Two of the offers were oral. 20.____
    In order to PROPERLY serve his employer, he must submit

    A. the offers in the order he received them
    B. only the written offer
    C. only those offers accompanied by a binder deposit
    D. all of the offers regardless of form, binder deposit, price, or order in which they were received

KEY (CORRECT ANSWERS)

1.	C	11.	D
2.	B	12.	B
3.	C	13.	B
4.	D	14.	D
5.	A	15.	D
6.	B	16.	D
7.	D	17.	D
8.	D	18.	C
9.	B	19.	D
10.	C	20.	D

TEST 2

DIRECTIONS: Each question or incomplete statement is followed by several suggested answers or completions. Select the one that BEST answers the question or completes the statement. *PRINT THE LETTER OF THE CORRECT ANSWER IN THE SPACE AT THE RIGHT.*

1. A contract with a promise of performance on one side is called a(n) _____ contract. 1.____

   A. implied
   B. bilateral
   C. executed
   D. unilateral

2. The passage or amendment of rules by the licensing commission is an exercise of which power? 2.____

   A. Executive
   B. Quasi-legislative
   C. Ministerial
   D. Quasi-judicial

3. Which of the following is probably NOT real estate? 3.____
   A

   A. tree
   B. refrigerator
   C. lease
   D. fence

4. Prior to acceptance of the offer, the earnest money deposit is under control of the 4.____

   A. broker
   B. seller
   C. broker and buyer-depositor
   D. buyer-depositor

5. A purchaser signs an offer stating that he wishes to offer $65,000 for a home listed for $67,000. His offer is accepted and signed by the offeree. Prior to being notified of the acceptance, the purchaser enters into an agreement to purchase another property. Which of the following applies? 5.____

   A. If the purchaser revokes the $65,000 offer prior to being notified of the acceptance of the offer, no breach of contract has occurred.
   B. The purchaser has breached the contract because offers must remain in effect for a reasonable length of time.
   C. The purchaser will be found guilty of fraud because this is a direct violation of the Statute of Frauds.
   D. Both B and C are correct.

6. If a seller of property did not receive all money due him and did not receive security for that unpaid money, he is eligible for a 6.____

   A. lis pendens
   B. second mortgage
   C. mechanic's lien
   D. vendor's lien

7. Which of the following business organizations can register as a broker? 7.____

   A. Corporation not for profit
   B. Corporation for profit
   C. Corporation sole
   D. Cooperative association

8. Broker A pays $50 for a 90-day option to owner Owen. The agreed-upon price is $100,000. On the 60th day, broker A finds a purchaser for the property at a sales price of $130,000. Broker A exercises his option and sells the property for $130,000. Which of the following applies?

   A. Broker A is entitled to a $30,000 profit
   B. Broker A has violated his fiduciary duties and is liable
   C. Broker A will have to share his profit
   D. None of the above

9. The right granted by a property owner to another to enter upon that owner's property is known as an

   A. encumbrance   B. easement
   C. encroachment   D. escheat

10. Real estate salesmen may be employed by

    A. owners *only*
    B. brokers *only*
    C. broker or owner-employer
    D. none of the above

11. A deed warranting title only against claims of the grantor, his heirs, assigns, executors, or administrators, and others claiming by or through him is called a _____ deed.

    A. general warranty   B. bargain and sale
    C. quit-claim   D. special warranty

12. Brokers A and B are partners in developing a parcel of land. C, a licensed salesperson, later purchases a share of the partnership. All proceeds from the sale of the developed land are divided according to ownership shares. Which of the following is CORRECT?

    A. C must be a broker to become a true partner.
    B. The salesperson must be inactive.
    C. No registration with the licensing commission is necessary.
    D. This partnership must register with the licensing commission.

13. In order to reduce the risk inherent in originating high loan-to-value ratio loans, lenders require

    A. increased interest rates   B. mortgage insurance
    C. discount   D. all of the above

14. Prior to the marriage, real estate owned by a husband or wife is presumed to be

    A. in a joint estate
    B. in a tenancy in common
    C. in an estate by the entireties
    D. separate property

15. The mortgagor's right to bring himself out of default by paying money owed to the lender is called

    A. the assumption of mortgage   B. the amortization of mortgage
    C. the equity of redemption   D. strict foreclosure

16. A mentally incompetent person may act as a grantor and deliver title to his own property by signing a _____ deed. 16._____

    A. guardian's
    B. committee's
    C. quit-claim
    D. none of the above

17. A member of the licensing commission may serve no more than _____ years. 17._____

    A. four
    B. eight
    C. ten
    D. none of the above

18. A written offer to purchase is submitted to a seller and he, in turn, changes the terms or conditions, initials the changes, signs the instrument, and sends it back to the offeror. In the law of contracts, this is a(n) 18._____

    A. offer
    B. binding offer
    C. irrevocable offer
    D. counteroffer

19. How many acres are contained in the N 1/2 of the SW 1/4 of the SE 1/4 of the NE 1/4 of Section 9? 19._____
    _____ acres.

    A. 10   B. 5   C. 2 1/2   D. 1 1/4

20. Negative taxable income is known as 20._____

    A. capital gain
    B. cash flow
    C. debt service
    D. tax shelter

KEY (CORRECT ANSWERS)

1.	D	11.	D
2.	B	12.	C
3.	B	13.	B
4.	D	14.	D
5.	A	15.	C
6.	D	16.	D
7.	B	17.	D
8.	B	18.	D
9.	B	19.	B
10.	C	20.	D

TEST 3

DIRECTIONS: Each question or incomplete statement is followed by several suggested answers or completions. Select the one that BEST answers the question or completes the statement. *PRINT THE LETTER OF THE CORRECT ANSWER IN THE SPACE AT THE RIGHT.*

1. During periods of disintermediation in the primary mortgage market, the mortgage money supply

    A. is unaffected
    B. decreases
    C. increases
    D. either increases or decreases, according to demand

2. Under the income approach to appraisal, value equals

    A. vacant land value plus depreciated building value
    B. rate times income
    C. rate divided by income
    D. income divided by rate

3. A and B form a business in which A is totally liable for any debts which are incurred, but B is only liable to the extent of his investment.
   This is PROBABLY a

    A. corporation   B. general partnership
    C. joint venture   D. limited partnership

4. Brokers are permitted to draw leases

    A. in the normal course of their business
    B. if power of attorney is granted to the owner
    C. never
    D. only if the brokers divest

5. The license of a broker is revoked.
   Licenses of salespeople employed by that broker are

    A. revoked   B. suspended
    C. reprimanded   D. canceled

6. Which of the following may involve the securities laws as well as the real estate laws?

    A. Condominiums
    B. Sales of real estate by transfer of stock of a corporation
    C. Group investment
    D. All of the above

7. Finders' fees paid to unlicensed individuals

    A. are illegal
    B. are simply poor business practices
    C. should be made to stimulate referrals
    D. are not illegal

8. Qualifying refers to

    A. lender analyzing borrower and property
    B. salesperson determining a prospect's needs and capabilities
    C. broker checking up on past clients
    D. both A and B

Questions 9-12.

DIRECTIONS: Questions 9 through 12 are to be answered on the basis of the following passage.

John is a salesperson working for Ann, the broker. John obtains a written offer and a deposit on a property listed with the office. He deposits the money in his own account, indicating that it is to be held in escrow for the buyer. The seller accepts the offer, and John writes a check to his broker for the deposit. She deposits the check in her business account. The buyer defaults, and Ann divides the escrow deposit with John.

9. What should John have done with the deposit money?

    A. Exactly what he did since the problem is the action taken by Ann, the broker
    B. Left it in his own escrow account
    C. Immediately turned it over to his broker
    D. Held it until the offer was accepted, then turned it over to his broker

10. What should Ann have done when she received the deposit?

    A. Exactly what she did since the buyer and seller agreed to it
    B. Immediately deposited it in her escrow account
    C. Returned the money to the buyer
    D. Left the money in John's escrow account

11. Which of the following is(are) CORRECT?
      I. John is guilty of conversion.
      II. Ann is guilty of conversion.

    The CORRECT answer is:

    A. I *only*
    B. II *only*
    C. Both I and II
    D. Neither I nor II

12. Assuming that the money had been handled properly up until the time of default by the buyer, what should Ann do upon the buyer's default?

    A. Return the deposit
    B. Exactly what she did
    C. Divide the money equally with John and the seller
    D. Divide the money with the seller according to their agreement and divide her share with John according to their agreement

13. A first-degree misdemeanor will be imposed by courts as a result of

    A. violations of advance fee accounting requirements or false advertising
    B. payment made from the Recovery Fund
    C. any violation of law
    D. B and C are correct

14. Owner A lists 1000 acres with broker B, and specifies the price and terms he will accept. B discovers that by selling on the price and terms stated, A will be liable for a large amount of income tax.
    B should

    A. change the listing for the protection of the principal
    B. tell A nothing because he has nothing to do with income tax
    C. follow the instructions of the principal
    D. advise A of this and tell him to seek the advice of an income tax expert

15. Which of the following shares of real property will a widow with no children receive at her husband's death in the absence of a will?

    A. One-third   B. All   C. One-half   D. None

16. An estate held by two or more parties in which each has equal or proportionate rights as to possession, enjoyment, and the time and duration, having the same or different origin, is being held as a(n)

    A. estate for years
    B. joint estate
    C. estate by the entireties
    D. tenancy in common

17. A seller agrees to deliver to a buyer a perfect record title. Examination of the abstract by a competent attorney reveals breaks in the chain of title.
    The seller would then do which of the following?

    A. Buy title insurance for the buyer
    B. File a suit to quiet title
    C. Get an affidavit from the Clerk of the Circuit Court attesting to his knowledge and belief that the seller's title is good
    D. Transfer title by quit-claim deed

18. A broker-salesperson employed by more than one owner should

    A. apply for a multiple license
    B. apply for a group license
    C. broker-salesperson may not be employed by an owner
    D. none of the above

19. If all rights under a lease are subrogated, the result is

    A. a sublease   B. an assignment
    C. a violation of law D. either A or B

20. A broker may collect a commission when he has negotiated a sale of property with the knowledge and consent of the owner even though no previous express listing was given the broker on the basis that he had a(n) 20.____

   A. open listing
   B. true option
   C. implied listing
   D. option which should be treated as a listing

KEY (CORRECT ANSWERS)

1.	B	11.	C
2.	D	12.	D
3.	D	13.	A
4.	C	14.	D
5.	D	15.	B
6.	D	16.	D
7.	A	17.	B
8.	D	18.	D
9.	C	19.	B
10.	B	20.	C

TEST 4

DIRECTIONS: Each question or incomplete statement is followed by several suggested answers or completions. Select the one that BEST answers the question or completes the statement. *PRINT THE LETTER OF THE CORRECT ANSWER IN THE SPACE AT THE RIGHT.*

1. If a grantor in a deed is insolvent, a quit-claim deed is as desirable as a _____ deed. 1.____

    A. bargain and sale
    B. special warranty
    C. general warranty
    D. all of the above

2. What is the government survey method description of the property shown at the right? 2.____

    A. NE 1/4 of the NE 1/4 of the SW 1/4 of Section 8
    B. NW 1/4 of the NW 1/4 of the SW 1/4 of Section 8
    C. N 1/2 of the NE 1/4 of the SE 1/4 of Section 8
    D. SW 1/4 of the NE 1/4 of the NE 1/4 of Section 8

    Section B

3. A violation of law may result in 3.____

    A. imprisonment
    B. injunction
    C. suspension
    D. all of the above

4. The mortgage lien remains in effect until 4.____

    A. the note is paid in full
    B. defeasance clause is satisfied
    C. a satisfaction is signed and recorded
    D. all of the above

5. An exclusive listing 5.____

    A. guarantees the listing broker a commission if the property is sold through another broker
    B. must be in writing
    C. is given to only one broker
    D. all of the above

6. A broker sells a prospective tenant a rental list for $100. The prospective tenant inspected all the properties and found them to be occupied. The tenant then demanded a full refund; what action should the broker take? 6.____

    A. Refund $100
    B. Refund $25
    C. Refund $75
    D. No refund should be made

7. A license is 7.____

    A. prima facie evidence of licensure
    B. issued for a period not to exceed two years
    C. proof of residency
    D. both A and B

8. B wants a motel site, and salesperson A showed him a good location which was zoned for a motel. A then went on vacation. Upon A's return, B purchased the site with A's assistance. A did not know that while he was on vacation the zoning had been changed, and B was subsequently denied a building permit for his motel.
   Which applies?

   A. A is guilty of nothing as there was no intent.
   B. A is guilty of negligence and may be disciplined.
   C. A and his broker are both guilty of fraud and may be disciplined.
   D. A is guilty of culpable negligence and subject to discipline.

9. When a broker represents two parties in a transaction,

   A. he must have the consent of both parties in order to collect a dual commission
   B. he must disclose his agency to both parties
   C. he may not represent two parties with adverse interests in a transaction
   D. both A and B are correct

10. When the license period is about to expire, the licensee should apply for a renewal. The effective date for that renewal will be the date

    A. the licensee makes the proper application to the department
    B. the department receives the application in proper form with proper fee attached
    C. following the expiration date of the original license
    D. the licensee receives the license

11. When a dispute arises concerning the disposition of escrowed funds and the broker is the escrow agent, the broker's FIRST action should be to

    A. ask the licensing commission for an Escrow Disbursement Order
    B. give the deposit to the seller
    C. collect his portion of the deposit as damages
    D. notify the licensing commission

12. Which of the following is(are) CORRECT?
    I. All officers and directors of real estate corporations must be brokers
    II. All partners in a real estate partnership must be brokers
    The CORRECT answer is:

    A. I only   B. II only
    C. Both I and II   D. Neither I nor II

13. Paul, a service station owner, has been appointed by a court to appraise another service station. Paul has no real estate license.
    Which of the following applies?

    A. He may apply to the licensing commission for a special exception.
    B. He may appraise the property only if he is knowledgeable as to its value.
    C. He must appraise the property while under the supervision of a licensed real estate broker.
    D. He may be compensated for appraising the property.

14. Using borrowed money to finance the purchase of real estate is known as

    A. larceny
    B. conversion
    C. leverage
    D. commingling

15. A licensee who appeals a decision by the real estate commission regarding a disciplinary decision may have his license privileges restored by

    A. injunction
    B. warrant
    C. the hearing officer
    D. writ of mandamus

16. Concerning the collection of advance fees, the broker should place

    A. 75 percent in escrow to be used for the benefit of the principal
    B. 100 percent in escrow
    C. 25 percent in escrow to be used for the benefit of the principal
    D. 100 percent in escrow to be used for the benefit of the principal

17. In order for a salesperson to become a successful broker applicant, he must

    A. work for one active broker for one year as an active salesperson
    B. complete the required educational course for broker
    C. work for one active broker or an owner-employer for one year as an active salesperson
    D. both A and B are correct

18. Which of the following is(are) CORRECT?
    I. If the first mortgage is paid off and satisfied, the second mortgage becomes the first.
    II. Both husband and wife must execute a satisfaction of mortgage when the mortgage is held in the husband's name only.

    The CORRECT answer is:

    A. I *only*
    B. II *only*
    C. Both I and II
    D. Neither I nor II

19. Broker Alice and broker Bob formed a partnership to provide real estate services for others. Broker Alice converts funds and has her license suspended.
    Which applies?

    A. Listings held by the partnership have been terminated
    B. The partnership license has been canceled
    C. Salespeople working for the partnership should obtain a reissue of their license under a new employer if they desire to continue operating
    D. All of the above

20. A real estate salesperson wishes to incorporate to buy, develop, and sell real estate.
    Which of the following BEST applies?

    A. He must obtain a broker's license.
    B. He must register the corporation with the real estate commission.
    C. No license is necessary.
    D. Both A and B are correct.

KEY (CORRECT ANSWERS)

1.	D	11.	D
2.	A	12.	D
3.	D	13.	D
4.	C	14.	C
5.	C	15.	D
6.	A	16.	A
7.	D	17.	B
8.	D	18.	A
9.	C	19.	D
10.	C	20.	C

PREPARING WRITTEN MATERIALS

EXAMINATION SECTION
TEST 1

DIRECTIONS: Each question or incomplete statement is followed by several suggested answers or completions. Select the one that BEST answers the question or completes the statement. *PRINT THE LETTER OF THE CORRECT ANSWER IN THE SPACE AT THE RIGHT.*

Questions 1-21.

DIRECTIONS: In each of the following sentences, which were taken from students' transcripts, there may be an error. Indicate the appropriate correction in the space at the right. If the sentence is correct as is, indicate this choice. Unnecessary changes will be considered incorrect.

1. In that building there seemed to be representatives of Teachers College, the Veterans Bureau, and the Businessmen's Association.

   A. Teacher's College B. Veterans' Bureau
   C. Businessmens Association D. Correct as is

   1.____

2. In his travels, he visited St. Paul, San Francisco, Springfield, Ohio, and Washington, D.C.

   A. Ohio and B. Saint Paul
   C. Washington, D.C. D. Correct as is

   2.____

3. As a result of their purchasing a controlling interest in the syndicate, it was well-known that the Bureau of Labor Statistics' calculations would be unimportant.

   A. of them purchasing B. well known
   C. Statistics D. Correct as is

   3.____

4. Walter Scott, Jr.'s, attempt to emulate his father's success was doomed to failure.

   A. Junior's, B. Scott's, Jr.
   C. Scott, Jr.'s attempt D. Correct as is

   4.____

5. About B.C. 250 the Romans invaded Great Britain, and remains of their highly developed civilization can still be seen.

   A. 250 B.C. B. Britain and
   C. highly-developed D. Correct as is

   5.____

6. The two boss's sons visited the children's department.

   A. bosses B. bosses'
   C. childrens' D. Correct as is

   6.____

7. Miss Amex not only approved the report, but also decided that it needed no revision.

   A. report; but B. report but
   C. report. But D. Correct as is

   7.____

81

8. Here's brain food in a jiffy—economical, too!

   A. economical too!
   B. 'brain food'
   C. jiffy-economical
   D. Correct as is

9. She said, "He likes the "Gatsby Look" very much."

   A. said "He
   B. "he
   C. 'Gatsby Look'
   D. Correct as is

10. We anticipate that we will be able to visit them briefly in Los Angeles on Wednesday after a five-day visit.

    A. Wednes-
    B. 5 day
    C. five day
    D. Correct as is

11. She passed all her tests, and, she now has a good position.

    A. tests, and she
    B. past
    C. tests;
    D. Correct as is

12. The billing clerk said, "I will send the bill today"; however, that was a week ago, and it hasn't arrived yet!

    A. today;"
    B. today,"
    C. ago and
    D. Correct as is

13. "She types at more-than-average speed," Miss Smith said, "but I feel that it is a result of marvelous concentration and self control on her part."

    A. more than average
    B. "But
    C. self-control
    D. Correct as is

14. The state of Alaska, the largest state in the union, is also the northernmost state.

    A. Union
    B. Northernmost State
    C. State of Alaska
    D. Correct as is

15. The memoirs of Ex-President Nixon, according to figures, sold more copies than <u>Six Crises</u>, the book he wrote in the 60's.

    A. Six Crises
    B. ex-President
    C. 60s
    D. Correct as is

16. "There are three principal elements, determining the hazard of buildings: the contents hazard, the fire resistance of the structure, and the character of the interior finish," concluded the speaker.
    The one of the following statements that is MOST acceptable is that, in the above passage,

    A. the comma following the word *elements* is incorrect
    B. the colon following the word *buildings* is incorrect
    C. the comma following the word *finish* is incorrect
    D. there is no error in the punctuation of the sentence

17. He spoke on his favorite topic, "Why We Will Win." (How could I stop him?)

    A. Win".
    B. him?).
    C. him)?
    D. Correct as is

18. "All any insurance policy is, is a contract for services," said my insurance agent, Mr. Newton.

    A. Insurance Policy
    B. Insurance Agent
    C. policy is is a
    D. Correct as is

19. Inasmuch as the price list has now been up dated, we should send it to the printer.

    A. In as much
    B. updated
    C. pricelist
    D. Correct as is

20. We feel that "Our know-how" is responsible for the improvement in technical developments.

    A. "our
    B. know how
    C. that,
    D. Correct as is

21. Did Cortez conquer the Incas? the Aztecs? the South American Indians?

    A. Incas, the Aztecs, the South American Indians?
    B. Incas; the Aztecs; the South American Indians?
    C. south American Indians?
    D. Correct as is

22. Which one of the following forms for the typed name of the dictator in the closing lines of a letter is generally MOST acceptable in the United States?

    A. (Dr.) James F. Farley
    B. Dr. James F. Farley
    C. Mr. James F. Farley, Ph.D.
    D. James F. Farley

23. The plural of

    A. turkey is turkies
    B. cargo is cargoes
    C. bankruptcy is bankruptcys
    D. son-in-law is son-in-laws

24. The abbreviation *viz.* means MOST NEARLY

    A. namely
    B. for example
    C. the following
    D. see

25. In the sentence, *A man in a light-gray suit waited thirty-five minutes in the ante-room for the all-important document,* the word IMPROPERLY hyphenated is

    A. light-gray
    B. thirty-five
    C. ante-room
    D. all-important

KEY (CORRECT ANSWERS)

1.	D	11.	A
2.	C	12.	D
3.	B	13.	D
4.	D	14.	A
5.	A	15.	B
6.	B	16.	A
7.	B	17.	D
8.	D	18.	D
9.	C	19.	B
10.	C	20.	A

21.	D
22.	D
23.	B
24.	A
25.	C

TEST 2

DIRECTIONS: Each question or incomplete statement is followed by several suggested answers or completions. Select the one that BEST answers the question or completes the statement. *PRINT THE LETTER OF THE CORRECT ANSWER IN THE SPACE AT THE RIGHT.*

Questions 1-10.

DIRECTIONS: In each of the following groups of four sentences, one sentence contains an error in sentence structure, grammar, usage, diction, or punctuation. Indicate the INCORRECT sentence.

1. A. The lecture finished, the audience began asking questions.
   B. Any man who could accomplish that task the world would regard as a hero.
   C. Our respect and admiration are mutual.
   D. George did like his mother told him, despite the importunities of his playmates.

2. A. I cannot but help admiring you for your dedication to your job.
   B. Because they had insisted upon showing us films of their travels, we have lost many friends whom we once cherished.
   C. I am constrained to admit that your remarks made me feel bad.
   D. My brother having been notified of his acceptance by the university of his choice, my father immediately made plans for a vacation.

3. A. In no other country is freedom of speech and assembly so jealously guarded.
   B. Being a beatnik, he felt that it would be a betrayal of his cause to wear shoes and socks at the same time.
   C. Riding over the Brooklyn Bridge gave us an opportunity to see the Manhattan skyline.
   D. In 1961, flaunting SEATO, the North Vietnamese crossed the line of demarcation.

4. A. I have enjoyed the study of the Spanish language not only because of its beauty and the opportunity it offers to understand the Hispanic culture but also to make use of it in the business associations I have in South America.
   B. The opinions he expressed were decidedly different from those he had held in his youth.
   C. Had he actually studied, he certainly would have passed.
   D. A supervisor should be patient, tactful, and firm.

5. A. At this point we were faced with only three alternatives: to push on, to remain where we were, or to return to the village.
   B. We had no choice but to forgive so venial a sin.
   C. In their new picture, the Warners are flouting tradition.
   D. Photographs taken revealed that 2.5 square miles had been burned.

6. A. He asked whether he might write to his friends.
    B. There are many problems which must be solved before we can be assured of world peace.
    C. Each person with whom I talked expressed his opinion freely.
    D. Holding on to my saddle with all my strength the horse galloped down the road at a terrifying pace.

    6.____

7. A. After graduating high school, he obtained a position as a runner in Wall Street.
    B. Last night, in a radio address, the President urged us to subscribe to the Red Cross.
    C. In the evening, light spring rain cooled the streets.
    D. "Un-American" is a word which has been used even by those whose sympathies may well have been pro-Nazi.

    7.____

8. A. It is hard to conceive of their not doing good work.
    B. Who won - you or I?
    C. He having read the speech caused much comment.
    D. Their finishing the work proves that it can be done.

    8.____

9. A. Our course of study should not be different now than it was five years ago.
    B. I cannot deny myself the pleasure of publicly thanking the mayor for his actions.
    C. The article on "Morale" has appeared in the Times Literary Supplement.
    D. He died of tuberculosis contracted during service with the Allied Forces.

    9.____

10. A. If it wasn't for a lucky accident, he would still be an office-clerk.
    B. It is evident that teachers need help.
    C. Rolls of postage stamps may be bought at stationery stores.
    D. Addressing machines are used by firms that publish magazines.

    10.____

11. The one of the following sentences which contains NO error in usage is:

    A. After the robbers left, the proprietor stood tied in his chair for about two hours before help arrived.
    B. In the cellar I found the watchmans' hat and coat.
    C. The persons living in adjacent apartments stated that they had heard no unusual noises.
    D. Neither a knife or any firearms were found in the room.

    11.____

12. The one of the following sentences which contains NO error in usage is:

    A. The policeman lay a firm hand on the suspect's shoulder.
    B. It is true that neither strength nor agility are the most important requirement for a good patrolman.
    C. Good citizens constantly strive to do more than merely comply the restraints imposed by society.
    D. Twenty years is considered a severe sentence for a felony.

    12.____

13. Select the sentence containing an adverbial objective.

    A. Concepts can only acquire content when they are connected, however indirectly, with sensible experience.
    B. The cloth was several shades too light to match the skirt which she had discarded.

    13.____

C. The Gargantuan Hall of Commons became a tri-daily horror to Kurt, because two youths discerned that he had a beard and courageously told the world about it.
D. Brooding morbidly over the event, Elsie found herself incapable of engaging in normal activity.

14. Select the sentence containing a verb in the subjunctive mood. 14.____

   A. Had he known of the new experiments with penicillin dust for the cure of colds, he might have been tempted to try them in his own office.
   B. I should be very much honored by your visit.
   C. Though he has one of the highest intelligence quotients in his group, he seems far below the average in actual achievement.
   D. Long had I known that he would be the man finally selected for such signal honors.

15. Select the sentence containing one (or more) passive perfect participle(s). 15.____

   A. Having been apprised of the consequences of his refusal to answer, the witness finally revealed the source of his information.
   B. To have been placed in such an uncomfortable position was perhaps unfair to a journalist of his reputation.
   C. When deprived of special immunity he had, of course, no alternative but to speak.
   D. Having been obdurate until now, he was reluctant to surrender under this final pressure exerted upon him.

16. Select the sentence containing a predicate nominative. 16.____

   A. His dying wish, which he expressed almost with his last breath, was to see that justice was done toward his estranged wife.
   B. So long as we continue to elect our officials in truly democratic fashion, we shall have the power to preserve our liberties.
   C. We could do nothing, at this juncture, but walk the five miles back to camp.
   D. There was the spaniel, wet and cold and miserable, waiting silently at the door.

17. Select the sentence containing exactly TWO adverbs. 17.____

   A. The gentlemen advanced with exasperating deliberateness, while his lonely partner waited.
   B. If you are well, will you come early?
   C. I think you have guessed right, though you were rather slow, I must say.
   D. The last hundred years have seen more change than a thousand years of the Roman Empire, than a hundred thousand years of the stone age.

Questions 18-24.

DIRECTIONS: Select the choice describing the error in the sentence.

18. If us seniors do not support school functions, who will? 18.____

   A. Unnecessary shift in tense
   B. Incomplete sentence
   C. Improper case of pronoun
   D. Lack of parallelism

19. The principal has issued regulations which, in my opinion, I think are too harsh.   19.____

    A. Incorrect punctuation
    B. Faulty sentence structure
    C. Misspelling
    D. Redundant expression

20. The freshmens' and sophomores' performances equaled those of the juniors and seniors.   20.____

    A. Ambiguous reference
    B. Incorrect placement of punctuation
    C. Misspelling of past tense
    D. Incomplete comparison

21. Each of them, Anne and her, is an outstanding pianist; I can't tell you which one is best.   21.____

    A. Lack of agreement
    B. Improper degree of comparison
    C. Incorrect case of pronoun
    D. Run-on sentence

22. She wears clothes that are more expensive than my other friends.   22.____

    A. Misuse of *than*
    B. Incorrect relative pronoun
    C. Shift in tense
    D. Faulty comparison

23. At the very end of the story it implies that the children's father died tragically.   23.____

    A. Misuse of *implies*
    B. Indefinite use of pronoun
    C. Incorrect spelling
    D. Incorrect possessive

24. At the end of the game both of us, John and me, couldn't scarcely walk because we were so tired.   24.____

    A. Incorrect punctuation
    B. Run-on sentence
    C. Incorrect case of pronoun
    D. Double negative

Questions 25-30.

DIRECTIONS: Questions 25 through 30 consist of a sentence lacking certain needed punctuation. Pick as your answer the description of punctuation which will CORRECTLY complete the sentence.

25. If you take the time to keep up your daily correspondence you will no doubt be most efficient.   25.____

    A. Comma only after *doubt*
    B. Comma only after *correspondence*
    C. Commas after *correspondence, will,* and *be*
    D. Commas after *if, correspondence,* and *will*

26. Because he did not send the application soon enough he did not receive the up to date copy of the book.   26.____

    A. Commas after *application* and *enough*, and quotation marks before *up* and after *date*
    B. Commas after *application* and *enough*, and hyphens between *to* and *date*
    C. Comma after *enough*, and hyphens between *up* and *to* and between *to* and *date*
    D. Comma after *application*, and quotation marks before *up* and after *date*

27. The coordinator requested from the department the following items a letter each week summarizing progress personal forms and completed applications for tests.   27.____

    A. Commas after *items* and *completed*
    B. Semi-colon after *items* and *progress*, comma after *forms*
    C. Colon after *items*, commas after *progress* and *forms*
    D. Colon after *items*, commas after *forms* and *applications*

28. The supervisor asked Who will attend the conference next month.   28.____

    A. Comma after *asked*, period after *month*
    B. Period after *asked*, question mark after *month*
    C. Comma after *asked*, quotation marks before *Who*, quotation marks after *month*, and question mark after the quotation marks
    D. Comma after *asked*, quotation marks before *Who*, question mark after *month*, and quotation marks after the question mark

29. When the statistics are collected, we will forward the results to you as soon as possible.   29.____

    A. Comma after *you*
    B. Commas after *forward* and *you*
    C. Commas after *collected*, *results*, and *you*
    D. Comma after *collected*

30. The ecology of our environment is concerned with mans pollution of the atmosphere.   30.____

    A. Comma after *ecology*
    B. Apostrophe after *n* and before *s* in *mans*
    C. Commas after *ecology* and *environment*
    D. Apostrophe after *s* in *mans*

KEY (CORRECT ANSWERS)

1.	D	16.	A
2.	A	17.	C
3.	D	18.	C
4.	A	19.	D
5.	B	20.	B
6.	D	21.	B
7.	A	22.	D
8.	C	23.	B
9.	A	24.	D
10.	A	25.	B
11.	C	26.	C
12.	D	27.	C
13.	B	28.	D
14.	A	29.	D
15.	A	30.	B

TEST 3

DIRECTIONS: Each question or incorrect statement is followed by several suggested answers or completions. Select the one that BEST answers the question or completes the statement. *PRINT THE LETTER OF THE CORRECT ANSWER IN THE SPACE AT THE RIGHT.*

Questions 1-6.

DIRECTIONS: From the four choices offered in Questions 1 through 6, select the one which is INCORRECT.

1. A. Before we try to extricate ourselves from this struggle in which we are now engaged in, we must be sure that we are not severing ties of honor and duty.
   B. Besides being an outstanding student, he is also a leader in school government and a trophy-winner in school sports.
   C. If the framers of the Constitution were to return to life for a day, their opinion of our amendments would be interesting.
   D. Since there are three m's in the word, it is frequently misspelled.

2. A. It was a college with an excellance beyond question.
   B. The coach will accompany the winners, whomever they may be.
   C. The dean, together with some other faculty members, is planning a conference.
   D. The jury are arguing among themselves.

3. A. This box is less nearly square than that one.
   B. Wagner is many persons' choice as the world's greatest composer.
   C. The habits of Copperheads are different from Diamond Backs.
   D. The teacher maintains that the child was insolent.

4. A. There was a time when the Far North was unknown territory. Now American soldiers manning radar stations there wave to Boeing jet planes zooming by overhead.
   B. Exodus, the psalms, and Deuteronomy are all books of the Old Testament.
   C. Linda identified her china dishes by marking their bottoms with india ink.
   D. Harry S. Truman, former president of the United States, served as a captain in the American army during World War I.

5. A. The sequel of their marriage was a divorce.
   B. We bought our car secondhand.
   C. His whereabouts is unknown.
   D. Jones offered to use his own car, providing the company would pay for gasoline, oil, and repairs.

6. A. I read Golding's "Lord of the Flies".
   B. The orator at the civil rights rally thrilled the audience when he said, "I quote Robert Burns's line, 'A man's a man for a' that."
   C. The phrase "producer to consumer" is commonly used by market analysts.
   D. The lawyer shouted, "Is not this evidence illegal?"

Questions 7-9.

DIRECTIONS: In answering Questions 7 through 9, mark the letter A if faulty because of incorrect grammar, mark the letter B if faulty because of incorrect punctuation, mark the letter C if correct.

7. Mr. Brown our accountant, will audit the accounts next week.   7.____

8. Give the assignment to whomever is able to do it most efficiently.   8.____

9. The supervisor expected either your or I to file these reports.   9.____

Questions 10-14.

DIRECTIONS: In each of the following groups of four sentences, one sentence contains an error in sentence structure, grammar, usage, diction, or punctuation. Indicate the INCORRECT sentence.

10. A. The agent asked, "Did you say, 'Never again?"   10.____
    B. Kindly let me know whether you can visit us on the 17th.
    C. "I cannot accept that!" he exploded. "Please show me something else."
    D. Ed, will you please lend me your grass shears for an hour or so.

11. A. Recalcitrant though he may have been, Alexander was wilfully destructive.   11.____
    B. Everybody should look out for himself.
    C. John is one of those students who usually spends most of his time in the principal's office.
    D. She seems to feel that what is theirs is hers.

12. A. Be he ever so much in the wrong, I'll support the man while deploring his actions.   12.____
    B. The schools' lack of interest in consumer education is shortsighted.
    C. I think that Fitzgerald's finest stanza is one which includes the reference to youth's "sweet-scented manuscript."
    D. I never would agree to Anderson having full control of the company's policies.

13. A. We had to walk about five miles before finding a gas station.   13.____
    B. The willful sending of a false alarm has, and may, result in homicide.
    C. Please bring that book to me at once!
    D. Neither my sister nor I am interested in bowling.

14. A. He is one of the very few football players who doesn't wear a helmet with a face guard.   14.____
    B. But three volunteers appeared at the recruiting office.
    C. Such consideration as you can give us will be appreciated.
    D. When I left them, the group were disagreeing about the proposed legislation.

Question 15.

DIRECTIONS: Question 15 contains two sentences concerning criminal law. The sentences could contain errors in English grammar or usage. A sentence does not contain an error simply because it could be written in a different manner. In answering this question, choose answer
- A. if only sentence I is correct
- B. if only sentence II is correct
- C. if both sentences are correct
- D. if neither sentence is correct

15. I. The use of fire or explosives to destroy tangible property is proscribed by the criminal mischief provisions of the Revised Penal Law.
 II. The defendant's taking of a taxicab for the immediate purpose of affecting his escape did not constitute grand larceny.

15.____

KEY (CORRECT ANSWERS)

1. A	6. A
2. B	7. B
3. C	8. A
4. B	9. A
5. D	10. A

11. C
12. D
13. B
14. A
15. A

PREPARING WRITTEN MATERIAL

PARAGRAPH REARRANGEMENT
COMMENTARY

The sentences which follow are in scrambled order. You are to rearrange them in proper order and indicate the letter choice containing the correct answer at the space at the right.

Each group of sentences in this section is actually a paragraph presented in scrambled order. Each sentence in the group has a place in that paragraph; no sentence is to be left out. You are to read each group of sentences and decide upon the best order in which to put the sentences so as to form as well-organized paragraph.

The questions in this section measure the ability to solve a problem when all the facts relevant to its solution are not given.

More specifically, certain positions of responsibility and authority require the employee to discover connections between events sometimes, apparently, unrelated. In order to do this, the employee will find it necessary to correctly infer that unspecified events have probably occurred or are likely to occur. This ability becomes especially important when action must be taken on incomplete information.

Accordingly, these questions require competitors to choose among several suggested alternatives, each of which presents a different sequential arrangement of the events. Competitors must choose the MOST logical of the suggested sequences.

In order to do so, they may be required to draw on general knowledge to infer missing concepts or events that are essential to sequencing the given events. Competitors should be careful to infer only what is essential to the sequence. The plausibility of the wrong alternatives will always require the inclusion of unlikely events or of additional chains of events which are NOT essential to sequencing the given events.

It's very important to remember that you are looking for the best of the four possible choices, and that the best choice of all may not even be one of the answers you're given to choose from.

There is no one right way to solve these problems. Many people have found it helpful to first write out the order of the sentences, as they would have arranged them, on their scrap paper before looking at the possible answers. If their optimum answer is there, this can save them some time. If it isn't, this method can still give insight into solving the problem. Others find it most helpful to just go through each of the possible choices, contrasting each as they go along. You should use whatever method feels comfortable, and works, for you.

While most of these types of questions are not that difficult, we've added a higher percentage of the difficult type, just to give you more practice. Usually there are only one or two questions on this section that contain such subtle distinctions that you're unable to answer confidently, and you then may find yourself stuck deciding between two possible choices, neither of which you're sure about.

PREPARING WRITTEN MATERIAL
EXAMINATION SECTION
TEST 1

DIRECTIONS: The following groups of sentences need to be arranged in an order that makes sense. Select the letter preceding the sequence that represents the *BEST sentence order.* PRINT THE LETTER OF THE CORRECT ANSWER IN THE SPACE AT THE RIGHT.

1.
   I. A large Naval station on Alameda Island, near Oakland, held many warships in port, and the War Department was worried that if the bridge were to be blown up by the enemy, passage to and from the bay would be hopelessly blocked.
   II. Though many skeptics were opposed to the idea of building such an enormous bridge, the most vocal opposition came from a surprising source: the United States War Department.
   III. The War Department's concerns led to a showdown at San Francisco City Hall between Strauss and the Secretary of War, who demanded to know what would happen if a military enemy blew up the bridge.
   IV. In 1933, by submitting a construction cost estimate of $17 million, an engineer named Joseph Strauss won the contract to build the Golden Gate Bridge of San Francisco, which would then become one of the world's largest bridges.
   V. Strauss quickly ended the debate by explaining that the Golden Gate Bridge was to be a suspension bridge, whose roadway would hang in the air from cables strung between two huge towers, and would immediately sink into three hundred feet of water if it were destroyed.

   The best order is
   A. II, III, I, IV, V
   B. I, II, III, V, IV
   C. IV, II, I, III, V
   D. IV, I, III, V, II

1._____

2.
I. Plastic surgeons have already begun to use virtual reality to map out the complex nerve and tissue structures of a particular patient's face, in order to prepare for delicate surgery.
II. A virtual reality program responds to these movements by adjusting the Images that a person sees on a screen or through goggles, thereby creating an "interactive" world in which a person can see and touch three-dimensional graphic objects.
III. No more than a computer program that is designed to build and display graphic images, the virtual reality program takes graphic programs a step further by sensing a person's head and body movements.
IV. The computer technology known as virtual reality, now in its very first stages of development, is already revolutionizing some aspects of contemporary life.
V. Virtual reality computers are also being used by the space program, most recently to simulate conditions for the astronauts who were launched on a repair mission to the Hubble telescope.

The best order is
A. IV, II, I, V, III
B. III, I, V, II, IV
C. IV, III, II, I, V
D. III, I, II, IV, V

3.
I. Before you plant anything, the soil in your plant bed should be carefully raked level, a small section at a time, and any clods or rocks that can't be broken up should be removed.
II. Your plant should be placed in a hole that will position it at the same level it was at the nursery, and a small indentation should be pressed into the soil around the plant in order to hold water near it roots.
III. Before placing the plant in the soil, lightly separate any roots that may have been matted together in the container, cutting away any thick masses that can't be separated, so that the remaining roots will be able to grow outward.
IV. After the bed is ready, remove your plant from its container by turning it upside down and tapping or pushing on the bottom — never remove it by pulling on the plant.
V. When you bring home a small plant in an individual container from the nursery, there are several things to remember while preparing to plant it in your own garden.

The best order is
A. V, IV, III, II, I
B. V, I, IV, III, II
C. I, IV, II, III, V
D. I, IV, V, II, III

4.
   I. The motte and its tower were usually built first, so that sentries could use it as a lookout to warn the castle workers of any danger that might approach the castle.
   II. Though the moat and palisade offered the bailey a good deal of protection, it was linked to the motte by a set of stairs that led to a retractable drawbridge at the motte's gate, to enable people to evacuate and retreat onto the motte in case of an attack.
   III. The *motte* of these early castles was a fortified hill, sometimes as high as one hundred feet, on which stood a palisade and tower.
   IV. The *bailey* was a clear, level spot below the motte, also enclosed by a palisade, which in turn was surrounded by a large trench or moat.
   V. The earliest castles built in Europe were not the magnificent stone giants that still tower over much of the European landscape, but simpler wooden constructions called motte-and-bailey castles.

The best order is
A. V, III, I, IV, II
B. V, IV, I, II, III
C. I, IV, IIII, II, V
D. I, III, II, IV, V

5.
   I. If an infant is left alone or abandoned for a short while, its immediate response is to cry loudly, accompanying its screams with aggressive flailing of its legs and limbs.
   II. If a child has been abandoned for a longer period of time, it becomes completely still and quiet, as if realizing that now its only chance for survival is to shut its mouth and remain motionless.
   III. Along with their intense fear of the dark, the crying behavior of human infants offers insights into how prehistoric newborn children might have evolved instincts that would prevent them from becoming victims of predators.
   IV. This behavior often surprises people who enter a hospital's maternity ward for the first time and encounter total silence from a roomful of infants.
   V. This violent screaming response is quite different from an infant's cries of discomfort or hunger, and seems to serve as either the child's first line of defense against an unwanted intruder, or a desperate attempt to communicate its position to the mother.

The best order is
A. III, II, IV, I, V
B. III, I, V, II, IV
C. I, V, IV, II, III
D. II, IV, I, V, III

6.
   I. When two cats meet who are strangers, their first actions and gestures determine who the "dominant" cat will be, at least for the time being.
   II. Unlike dogs, cats are typically a solitary animal species who avoid social interaction, but they do display specific social responses to each other upon meeting.
   III. This is unlikely, however; before such a point of open hostility is reached, one of the cats will usually take the "submissive" position of crouching down while looking away from the other cat.
   IV. If a cat desires dominance or sees the other cat as a threat to its territory, it will stare directly at the intruder with a lowered tail.
   V. If the other cat responds with a similar gesture, or with the strong defensive posture of an arched back, laid-back ears and raised tail, a fight or chase is likely if neither cat gives in.

   The best order is
   A. IV, II, I, V, III
   B. I, II, IV, V, III
   C. I, IV, V, III, II
   D. II, I, IV, V, III

7.
   I. A star or planet's gravitational force can best be explained in this way: anything passing through this "dent" in space will veer toward the star or planet as if it were rolling into a hole.
   II. Objects that are massive or heavy, such as stars or planets, "sink" into this surface, creating a sort of dent or concavity in the surrounding space.
   III. Black holes, the most massive objects known to exist in space, create dents so large and deep that the space surrounding them actually folds in on itself, preventing anything that falls in — even light — from ever escaping again.
   IV. The sort of dent a star or planet makes depends on how massive it is; planets generally have weak gravitational pulls, but stars, which are larger and heavier, make a bigger "dent" that will attract more matter.
   V. In outer space, the force of gravity works as if the surrounding space is a soft, flat surface.

   The best order is
   A. III, V, II, I, IV
   B. III, IV, I, V, II
   C. V, II, I, IV, III
   D. I, V, II, IV, III

8.
- I. Eventually, the society of Kyoto gave the world one of its first and greatest novels when Japan's most prominent writer, Lady Murasaki Shikibu, wrote her chronicle of Kyoto's society, *The Tale of Genji*, which preceded the first European novels by more than 500 years.
- II. The society of Kyoto was dedicated to the pleasures of art; the courtiers experimented with new and colorful methods of sculpture, painting, writing, decorative gardening, and even making clothes.
- III. Japanese culture began under the powerful authority of Chinese Buddhism, which influenced every aspect of Japanese life from religion to politics and art.
- IV. This new, vibrant culture was so sophisticated that all the people in Kyoto's imperial court considered themselves poets, and the line between life and art hardly existed — lovers corresponded entirely through written verses, and even government officials communicated by writing poems to each other.
- V. In the eighth century, when the emperor established the town of Kyoto as the capital of the Japanese empire, Japanese society began to develop its own distinctive style.

The best order is
A. V, II, IV, I, III
B. II, I, V, IV, III
C. V, III, IV, I, II
D. III, V, II, IV, I

9.
- I. Instead of wheels, the HSST uses two sets of magnets, one which sits on the track, and another that is carried by the train; these magnets generate an identical magnetic field which forces the two sets apart.
- II. In the last few decades, railway travel has become less popular throughout the world, because it is much slower than travel by airplane, and not much less expensive.
- III. The HSST's designers say that the train can take passengers from one town to another as quickly as a jet plane — while consuming less than half the energy.
- IV. This repellent effect is strong enough to lift the entire train above the trackway, and the train, literally traveling on air, rockets along at speeds of up to 300 miles per hour.
- V. The revolutionary technology of magnetic levitation, currently being tested by Japan's experimental HSST (High Speed Surface Transport), may yet bring passenger trains back from the dead.

The best order is
A. II, V, I, IV, III
B. II, I, IV, III, V
C. V, II, III, I, IV
D. V, I, III, IV, II

10.
- I. When European countries first began to colonize the African continent, their impression of the African people was of a vast group of loosely organized tribal societies, without any great centralized source of power or wealth.
- II. The legend of Timbuktu persisted until the nineteenth century, when a French adventurer visited Timbuktu and found that raids by neighboring tribesmen had made the city a shadow of its former self.
- III. In the fifteenth century, when the stories of travelers who had traveled Africa's Sudan region began circulating around Europe, this impression began to change.
- IV. In 1470, an Italian merchant named Benedetto Dei traveled to Timbuktu and confirmed these rumors, describing a thriving metropolis where rich and poor people worshipped together in the city's many ornate mosques — there was even a university in Timbuktu, much like its European counterparts, where African scholars pursued their studies in the arts and sciences.
- V. The travelers' legends told of an enormous city in the western Sudan, Timbuktu, where the streets were crowded with goods brought by faraway caravans, and where there was a stone palace as large as any in Europe.

The best order is
A. III, V, I, IV, II
B. I, II, IV, III, V
C. I, III, V, IV, II
D. II, I, III, IV, V

11.
- I. Also, our reference points in sighting the moon may make us believe that its size is changing; when the moon is rising through the trees, it seems huge, because our brains unconsciously compare the size of the moon with the size of the trees in the foreground.
- II. To most people, the sky itself appears more distant at the horizon than directly overhead, and if the moon's size — which remains constant — is projected from the horizon, the apparent distance of the horizon makes the moon look bigger.
- III. Up higher in the sky, the moon is set against tiny stars in the background, which will make the moon seem smaller.
- IV. People often wonder why the moon becomes bigger when it approaches the horizon, but most scientists agree that this is a complicated optical illusion, produced by at least three factors.
- V. The moon illusion may also be partially explained by a phenomenon that has nothing to do with errors in our perception — light that enters the earth's atmosphere is sometimes refracted, and so the atmosphere may act as a kind of magnifying glass for the moon's image.

The best order is
A. IV, III, V, II, I
B. IV, II, I, III, V
C. V, II, I, III, IV
D. II, I, III, IV, V

12.

I. When the Native Americans were introduced to the horses used by white explorers, they were amazed at their new alternative — here was an animal that was strong and swift, would patiently carry a person or other loads on its back, and, they later discovered, was right at home on the plains.
II. Before the arrival of European explorers to North America, the natives of the American plains used large dogs to carry their travois-long lodgepoles loaded with clothing, gear, and food.
III. These horses, it is now known, were not really strangers to North America; the very first horses originated here, on this continent, tens of thousands of years ago, and migrated into Asia across the Bering Land Bridge, a strip of land that used to link our continent with the Eastern world.
IV. At first, the natives knew so little about horses that at least one tribe tried to feed their new animals pieces of dried meat and animal fat, and were surprised when the horses turned their heads away and began to eat the grass of the prairie.
V. The American horse eventually became extinct, but its Asian cousins were reintroduced to the New World when the European explorers brought them to live among the Native Americans.

The best order is
A. II, I, IV, III, V
B. II, IV, I, III, V
C. I, II, IV, III, V
D. I, III, V, II, IV

13.

I. The dress worn by the dancer is believed to have been adorned in the past by shells which would strike each other as the dancer performed, creating a lovely sound.
II. Today's jingle-dress is decorated with the tin lids of snuff cans, which are rolled into cones and sewn onto the dress.
III. During the jingle-dress dance, the dancer must blend complicated footwork with a series of gentle hops that cause the cones to jingle in rhythm to a drumbeat.
IV. When contemporary Native American tribes meet for a pow-wow, one of the most popular ceremonies to take place is the women's jingle-dress dance.
V. Besides being more readily available than shells, the lids are thought by many dancers to create a softer, more subtle sound.

The best order is
A. II, IV, V, I, III
B. IV, II, I, III, V
C. II, I, III, V, IV
D. IV, I, II, V, III

14.
- I. If a homeowner lives where seasonal climates are extreme, deciduous shade trees — which will drop their leaves in the winter and allow sunlight to pass through the windows — should be planted near the southern exposure in order to keep the house cool during the summer.
- II. This trajectory is shorter and lower in the sky than at any other time of year during the winter, when a house most requires heating; the northern-facing parts of a house do not receive any direct sunlight at all.
- III. In designing an energy-efficient house, especially in colder climates, it is important to remember that most of the house's windows should face south.
- IV. Though the sun always rises in the east and sets in the west, the sun of the northern hemisphere is permanently situated in the southern portion of the sky.
- V. The explanation for why so many architects and builders want this "southern exposure" is related to the path of the sun in the sky.

The best order is
A. III, I, V, IV, II
B. III, V, IV, II, I
C. I, III, IV, II, V
D. I, II, V, IV, III

15.
- I. His journeying lasted twenty-four years and took him over an estimated 75,000 miles, a distance that would not be surpassed by anyone other than Magellan — who sailed around the world — for another six hundred years.
- II. Perhaps the most far-flung of these lesser-known travelers was Ibn Batuta, an African Moslem who left his birthplace of Tangier in the summer of 1325.
- III. Ibn Batuta traveled all over Africa and Asia, from Niger to Peking, and to the islands of Maldive and Indonesia.
- IV. However, a few explorers of the Eastern world logged enough miles and adventures to make Marco Polo's voyage look like an evening stroll.
- V. In America, the most well-known of the Old World's explorers are usually Europeans such as Marco Polo, the Italian who brought many elements of Chinese culture to the Western world.

The best order is
A. V, IV, II, III, I
B. V, IV, III, II, I
C. III, II, I, IV, V
D. II, III, I, IV, V

16.
- I. In the rain forests of South America, a rare species of frog practices a reproductive method that is entirely different from this standard process.
- II. She will eventually carry each of the tadpoles up into the canopy and drop each into its own little pool, where it will be easy to locate and safe from most predators.
- III. After fertilization, the female of the species, who lives almost entirely on the forest floor, lays between 2 and 16 eggs among the leaf litter at the base of a tree, and stands watch over these eggs until they hatch.
- IV. Most frogs are pond-dwellers who are able to deposit hundreds of eggs in the water and then leave them alone, knowing that enough eggs have been laid to insure the survival of some of their offspring.
- V. Once the tadpoles emerge, the female backs in among them, and a tadpole will wriggle onto her back to be carried high into the forest canopy, where the female will deposit it in a little pool of water cupped in the leaf of a plant.

The best order is
A. I, IV, III, II, V
B. I, III, V, II, IV
C. IV, III, II, V, I
D. IV, I, III, V, II

17.
- I. Eratosthenes had heard from travelers that at exactly noon on June 21, in the ancient city of Aswan, Egypt, the sun cast no shadow in a well, which meant that the sun must be directly overhead.
- II. He knew the sun always cast a shadow in Alexandria, and so he figured that if he could measure the length of an Alexandria shadow at the time when there was no shadow in Aswan, he could calculate the angle of the sun, and therefore the circumference of the earth.
- III. The evidence for a round earth was not new in 1492; in fact, Eratosthenes, an Alexandrian geographer who lived nearly sixteen centuries before Columbus's voyage (275-195 B.C.), actually developed a method for calculating the circumference of the earth that is still in use today.
- IV. Eratosthenes's method was correct, but his result — 28,700 miles — was about 15 percent too high, probably because of the inaccurate ancient methods of keeping time, and because Aswan was not due south of Alexandria, as Eratosthenes had believed.
- V. When Christopher Columbus sailed across the Atlantic Ocean for the first time in 1492, there were still some people in the world who ignored scientific evidence and believed that the earth was flat, rather than round.

The best order is
A. I, II, V, III, IV
B. V, III, IV, I, II
C. V, III, I, II, IV
D. III, V, I, II, IV

18.
- I. The first name for the child is considered a trial naming, often impersonal and neutral, such as the Ngoni name *Chabwera*, meaning "it has arrived."
- II. This sort of name is not due to any parental indifference to the child, but is a kind of silent recognition of Africa's sometimes high infant death rate; most parents ease the pain of losing a child with the belief that it is not really a person until it has been given a final name.
- III. In many tribal African societies, families often give two different names to their children, at different periods in time.
- IV. After the trial naming period has subsided and it is clear that the child will survive, the parents choose a final name for the child, an act that symbolically completes the act of birth.
- V. In fact, some African first-given names are explicitly uncomplimentary, translating as "I am dead" or "I am ugly," in order to avoid the jealousy of ancestral spirits who might wish to take a child that is especially healthy or attractive.

The best order is
A. III, I, II, V, IV
B. III, IV, II, I, V
C. IV, III, I, II, V
D. IV, V, III, I, II

19.
- I. Though uncertain of the definite reasons for this behavior, scientists believe the birds digest the clay in order to counteract toxins contained in the seeds of certain fruits that are eaten by macaws.
- II. For example, all macaws flock to riverbanks at certain times of the year to eat the clay that is found in river mud.
- III. The macaws of South America are not only among the largest and most beautifully colored of the world's flying birds, but they are also one of the smartest.
- IV. It is believed that macaws are forced to resort to these toxic fruits during the dry season, when foods are more scarce.
- V. The macaw's intelligence has led to intense study by scientists, who have discovered some macaw behaviors that have not yet been explained.

The best order is
A. III, IV, I, II, V
B. III, V, II, I, IV
C. V, II, I, IV, III
D. IV, I, II, III, V

20.
- I. Although Maggie Kuhn has since passed away, the Gray Panthers are still waging a campaign to reinstate the historical view of the elderly as people whose experience allows them to make their greatest contribution in their later years.
- II. In 1972, an elderly woman named Maggie Kuhn responded to this sort of treatment by forming a group called the Gray Panthers, an organization of both old and young adults with the common goal of creating change.
- III. This attitude is reflected strongly in the way elderly people are treated by our society; many are forced into early retirement, or are placed in rest homes in which they are isolated from their communities.
- IV. Unlike most other cultures around the world, Americans tend to look upon old age with a sense of dread and sadness.
- V. Kuhn believed that when the elderly are forced to withdraw into lives that lack purpose, society loses one of its greatest resources: people who have a lifetime of experience and wisdom to offer their communities.

The best order is
A. IV, III, II, V, I
B. IV, II, I, III, V
C. II, IV, III, V, I
D. II, I, IV, III, V

21.
- I. The current theory among most anthropologists is that humans evolved from apes who lived in trees near the grasslands of Africa.
- II. Still, some anthropologists insist that such an invention was necessary for the survival of early humans, and point to the Kung Bushmen of central Africa as a society in which the sling is still used in this way.
- III. Two of these inventions — fire, and weapons such as spears and clubs — were obvious defenses against predators, and there is archaeological evidence to support the theory of their use.
- IV. Once people had evolved enough to leave the safety of trees and walk upright, they needed the protection of several inventions in order to survive.
- V. But another invention, a leather or fiber sling that allowed mothers to carry children while leaving their hands free to gather roots or berries, would certainly have decomposed and left behind no trace of itself.

The best order is
A. I, II, III, V, IV
B. IV, I, II, III, V
C. I, IV, III, V, II
D. IV, III, V, II, I

22.
  I. The person holding the bird should keep it in hot water up to its neck, and the person cleaning should work a mild solution of dishwashing liquid into the bird's plumage, paying close attention to the head and neck.
  II. When rinsing the bird, after all the oil has been removed, the running water should be directed against the lay of its feathers, until water begins to bead off the surface of the feathers — a sign that all the detergent has been rinsed out.
  III. If you have rescued a sea bird from an oil spill and want to restore it to clean and normal living, you need a large sink, a constant supply of running hot water (a little over 100° F), and regular dishwashing liquid.
  IV. This cleaning with detergent solution should be repeated as many times as it takes to remove all traces of oil from the bird's feathers, sometimes over a period of several days.
  V. But before you begin to clean the bird, you must first find a partner, because cleaning an oiled bird is a two-person job.

The best order is
A. III, I, II, IV, V
B. III, V, I, IV, II
C. III, I, IV, V, II
D. III, IV, V, I, II

23.
  I. The most difficult time of year for the Tsaatang is the spring calving, when the reindeer leave their wintering ground and rush to their accustomed calving place, without stopping by night or by day.
  II. Reindeer travel in herds, and though some animals are tamed by the Tsaatang for riding or milking, the herds are allowed to roam free.
  III. This journey is hard for the Tsaatang, who carry all their possessions with them, but once it's over it proves worthwhile; the Tsaatang can immediately begin to gather milk from reindeer cows who have given birth.
  IV. The Tsaatang, a small tribe who live in the far northwest corner of Mongolia, practice a lifestyle that is completely dependent on the reindeer, their main resource for food, clothing, and transport.
  V. The people must follow their yearly migrations, living in portable shelters that resemble Native American tepees.

The best order is
A. I, III, II, V, IV
B. I, IV, II, V, III
C. IV, I, III, V, II
D. IV, II, V, I, III

24.

 I. The Romans later improved this system by installing these heated pipe networks throughout walls and ceilings, supplying heat to even the uppermost floors of a building — a system that, to this day, hasn't been much improved.
 II. Air-conditioning, the method by which humans control indoor temperatures, was practiced much earlier than most people think.
 III. The earliest heating devices other than open fires were used in 350 B.C. by the ancient Greeks, who directed air that had been heated by underground fires into baked clay pipes that ran under the floor.
 IV. Ironically, the first successful cooling system, patented in England in 1831, used fire as its main energy source — fires were lit in the attic of a building, creating an updraft of air that drew cool air into the building through ducts that had underground openings near the river Thames.
 V. Cooling buildings was more of a challenge, and wasn't attempted until 1500: a water-based system, designed by Leonardo da Vinci, does not appear to have been successful, since it was never used again.

The best order is
A. III, V, IV, I, II
B. III, I, II, V, IV
C. II, III, I, V, IV
D. IV, II, III, I, V

24._____

25.

 I. Cold, dry air from Canada passes over the Rocky Mountains and sweeps down onto the plains, where it collides with warm, moist air from the waters of the Gulf of Mexico, and when the two air masses meet, the resulting disturbance sometimes forms a violent funnel cloud that strikes the earth and destroys virtually everything in its path.
 II. Hurricanes, storms which are generally not this violent and last much longer, are usually given names by meteorologists, but this tradition cannot be applied to tornados, which have a life span measured in minutes and disappear in the same way as they are born — unnamed.
 III. A tornado funnel forms rotating columns of air whose speed reaches three hundred miles an hour — a speed that can only be estimated, because no wind-measuring devices in the direct path of a storm have ever survived.
 IV. The natural phenomena known as tornados occur primarily over the midwestern grasslands of the United States.
 V. It is here, meteorologists tell us, that conditions for the formation of tornados are sometimes perfect during the spring months.

The best order is
A. II, IV, V, I, III
B. II, III, I, V, IV
C. IV, V, I, III, II
D. IV, III, I, V, II

25._____

KEY (CORRECT ANSWERS)

1.	C	11.	B
2.	C	12.	A
3.	B	13.	D
4.	A	14.	B
5.	B	15.	A
6.	D	16.	D
7.	C	17.	C
8.	D	18.	A
9.	A	19.	B
10.	C	20.	A

21. C
22. B
23. D
24. C
25. C

AN HISTORIC LOOK AT REAL PROPERTY TAX ASSESSMENTS IN NEW YORK

CONTENTS

	Page
How the Property Tax Bill is Determined	1
Total Tax Levies	2
Assessed Value	2
Equalization Rates	3
Property Appraisal	3
Equalizing to Full Value	4
Importance of Accurate Equalization Rates	6
Property Subject to Tax	6
Full Value Assessment	7
Computer-Assisted Assessments	9
Assessors	10
Taxpayer Complaint and Appeal Provisions	11
Some Implications for Assessing Units	12
County and State Services for Local Assessors	13
County Services	13
State Services	14
The Gap Between Law and Practice	14
Conclusion	15

AN HISTORIC LOOK AT REAL PROPERTY TAX ASSESSMENTS IN NEW YORK

The property tax bill—its amount and the fairness with which it is shared—has been a public issue for apparently as long as we have had such a tax. Its history in New York goes back to early colonial times.

A combination of events in the late 70s has pushed the issue forward again as an important public question that is likely to be debated for at least the next few years. Among the events are recent New York court decisions that appear to require a major overhaul of property assessment practices and may substantially alter the distribution of property taxes among taxpayers.

The real property tax remains the most important and continuing source of revenues raised by local governments. It has come to be exceeded in New York by the totals of state and federal aid received by these local governments. Federal and state taxes, which do not include the property tax, have become several times larger than local collections. The property tax thus plays a much less important part in the total tax picture—federal, state, and local—than it did earlier in the century. Real property tax collections in New York State have long been rising, however, and still exceed those of either the state personal income tax or state and local sales taxes.[1]

A thorough study of why property taxes have increased is beyond the scope of this discussion, but a few reasons may be mentioned. Local governmental expenditures have expanded even more than revenues from these taxes. Wages, salaries, and fringe benefits of employees, and the prices of materials and supplies have increased. Payments to aid the needy and sick have moved up as the cost of living and of medical care have risen. The introduction of new functions and the expansion of existing ones in response to public demand have added to local tax requirements. These changes have taken place against an economic background of growing incomes for most individuals and families and of rising market values for most real estate.

As property taxes have increased and property values have risen, issues relating to assessment or valuation of property for tax purposes have become more acute. Assessment changes tend to lag behind changes in the market. All properties or types of property have not shared in rising market values to the same degree. As a result, assessed values, which probably never have reflected real values accurately in most communities, have become more and more remotely related to current conditions. Even if properties once were assessed with reasonable equity in relation to one another, a long lag in adjusting assessments to changing values usually produces substantial inequities among property taxpayers.

HOW THE PROPERTY TAX BILL IS DETERMINED

Three factors influence the amount of property taxes that a property owner pays. They are:
1. The total amount of taxes levied by local authorities.
2. The assessed value placed on the property as compared with all other taxable properties in a town (or other assessing district).
3. The equalization rates fixed by the state and the county.

---

[1] For 1975, revenues from the property tax were $6.7 billion; from income tax, $5.4 billion; and from sales tax, $3.5 billion. In 2017 they were, respectively: $2.4 billion; $51.5 billion; and from sales tax plus excise and user taxes, $15.7 billion.

Total Tax Levies

Three "layers" of local government cover New York State and are supported in part by the property tax. In addition, other local governments may be supported, depending upon where the property is located.

The state outside of New York City is divided into 57 counties. Each county is divided into towns, or towns and cities. The state is also divided into school districts. Property is therefore located in (1) a county, (2) a town or city, and (3) a school district.

One or more incorporated villages may be in a town. Special taxing or improvement districts also are laid out in many towns for fire protection, water supply, street lighting, and the like. Property in villages or districts helps to support the services provided.

Generally, property taxes are included in budgets that the local governments prepare. The amount of tax is usually determined by the difference between estimated expenditures for the coming year and estimated receipts from sources other than the property tax.

Passing judgment upon budgets and levying property taxes usually are the responsibility of local governing bodies, with the important qualification that they must abide by the requirements of state laws and the State Constitution. The more important governing bodies in rural areas are the town board, the county board (variously named county legislature board of supervisors, or board of representatives), the school board and annual school district meeting, and the village board of trustees.

These governing bodies, not the assessors, determine the total amount of property taxes needed.

Assessed Value

The work of the assessors is essentially concerned with dividing among individual property owners the total amounts of taxes that are levied by other authorities. The assessors do this by placing a value upon each property in their assessing district (in rural areas, principally the town).

Let us use a greatly simplified example. Suppose a town needs $300 of property taxes to help meet expenses for the coming year. There are three properties in the town. The assessor has assessed or valued each one at $10,000. The total assessed value is then $30,000. The rate required to yield the $300 is $10 per $1,000 of assessed value or 10 mills per dollar ($300 divided by $30,000). A $10 per $1,000 tax rate on property assessed at $10,000 yields $100. The $300 tax levy for town purposes is divided equally among the three properties because each is assessed at the same figure.

If one property were assessed at $15,000, another at $5,000, and the third at $10,000 the total assessed value would be the same, and so would the tax rate, but the taxes payable on the first property would be $150; on the second, $50; and on the third, $100. The taxes have been divided differently by changing the relationship between the assessed value on two properties as compared with the total assessed value.

We may, therefore, conclude that once the total amount of the town tax levy is determined the share of the tax that is payable on a piece of property depends on the assessed value placed on that property compared with the total valuation in the town.

Note that the tax payable does not depend on the assessed value of the property alone, but also upon the total valuation in the town. The assessed value on a piece of property may be changed without changing the amount of tax if the total assessed value in the town is changed to the same degree. To illustrate, let us return to the example above where the three properties in a town are assessed at $10,000 each. Suppose the assessor doubles the $10,000 assessment on one of the properties and changes the assessment on the others so that the total assessed valuation in the town is also doubled. The total value is then $60,000. The tax rate required to yield $300 is then cut in half to $5 per $1,000 of assessed value ($300 divided by $60,000). A $5 tax rate on the new assessment of $20,000 yields the same tax as before, or $100.

Often this important fact is not understood. The assessor of a town may attempt to raise the general level of assessments in order to bring them more nearly into line with realistic levels of value. Protests often follow, partly because of the apparently widespread belief that raising the assessed value on a property necessarily involves increased taxes.

Increased taxes on a property result only if the total levy is increased or if the assessed value of the property is aided by a greater percentage than the total valuation. Assume that the assessed values of $10,000 each for the three properties in the example are changed to $30,000, $20,000, and $10,000. The total assessed value has been doubled, from $30,000 to $60,000. The tax rate needed to raise $300 has been halved from $10 to $5 per $1,000 of assessed value. The original tax of $100 payable on each property has been changed to $150 for the first, $100 for the second, and $50 for the third. Taxes against the first property have increased because its assessed value was tripled while the total was doubled. Taxes payable on the second property remain unchanged because its assessed value was increased at the same rate as the total assessed value. Taxes due on the third property are reduced because its assessed value was not changed while the total assessed value for the town was doubled.

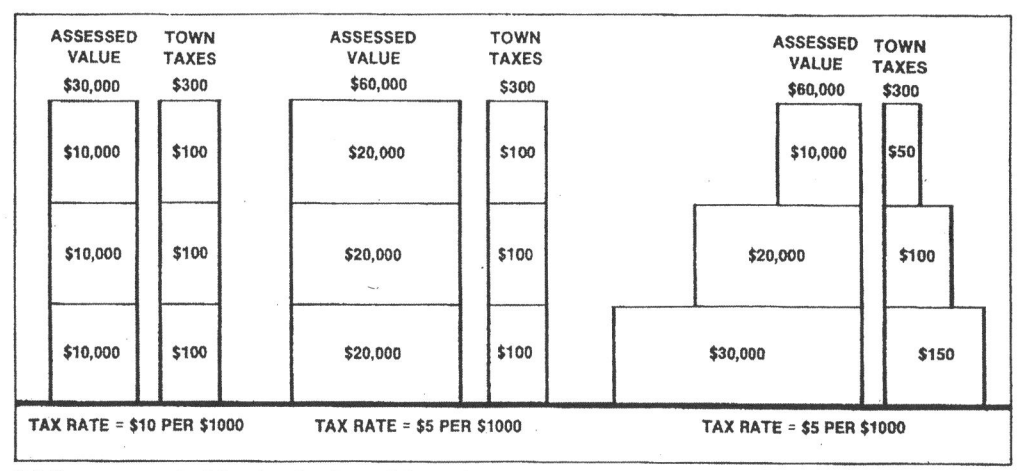

Relative assessments determine the share of the total property tax bill each individual pays.
The assessor's work essentially is to divide tax levies among taxpayers. Increased assessments do not necessarily mean increased taxes.

Equalization Rates

The Real Property Tax Law of New York (Section 306) requires that property be assessed at its full value. A common concept of full value in court decisions is the price at which a property would change hands under ordinary circumstances between a buyer who is willing but not compelled to buy and a seller who is willing but not compelled to sell. Full value thus is market value. Such a definition of full value cannot apply in all cases such as those involving highly specialized industrial properties which do not ordinarily change hands in the market. It is, however, applicable for more common types of property for which there is a market.

Property Appraisal. Placing a value on a property ultimately involves a subjective judgment by the appraiser. Well-established procedures are available, however, to make this decision as objective as possible. The three generally accepted methods of appraisal include not only the market approach, but also the income approach, but also the income approach and the cost approach.[2]

In the market approach, value is estimated by comparing the property with similar properties that have been sold recently (known by appraisers as "comparable sales"). The market approach approximates a value based on the amount a willing buyer would pay and a willing seller would take, neither being under undue pressure ("arm's-length sale"). Adjustments must be made for important differences between the property being appraised and the "comparable sales." This approach is useful and generally accurate when the market is active enough to make meaningful comparisons, and properties are fairly similar in nature, such as single family residences. A major limitation is the availability of comparable sales.

The income approach estimates values by treating the income earned or rental value of a property as a return on its capital value. Several methods are used to estimate property values through income capitalization. The reliability of this approach depends on the accuracy of income and rent as an indication of value and the extent to which the capitalization process actually exists in the market place. The value of a dairy farm, for example, may be estimated partly by the number of cows it will carry, and the income thereby yielded.

The third method of appraisal is the cost approach. The value of land must be estimated separately, using either the market or income approach. The replacement cost for new structures is estimated and then depreciated for loss in value over time. The depreciated value of buildings and structures is then added to the value of the land to provide an estimate for the parcel. The cost approach has many serious limitations, but is often used when adequate sales and income data are unavailable, such as for a section of a railroad, a power line facility, or a steel rolling mill of a complex corporation.

In actual practice, a careful appraiser or assessor may use a combination of these three approaches when the information is available. Where the real estate market is active and considerable construction is occurring, assessors may check their judgments on market value of a property against what they know about current construction costs, and may also estimate on the basis of potential rental or income value.

Equalizing to Full Value. Notwithstanding the Real Property Tax Law, most properties are assessed at less than full value in the great majority of assessing jurisdictions in New York. Further, wide variation exists in the average level or percentage of full value at which assessors in different districts assess property. To correct for these variations, the law provides that adjustments shall be made in specified situations where equitable allocation of the tax burden is affected. The adjustments are made by means of an equalization rate. The rate is simply a percentage figure that is expected to represent the average percentage of full value at which the assessor in an assessing district, such as a town, values properties.

The same law (Section 202 and Article 12) requires that the State Board of Equalization and Assessment establish sate equalization rates for each county, town, city, and village. To establish these rates, the Board regularly conducts market-value surveys on a sample of properties in each district and obtains information concerning valid, "arm's-length" sales of real estate.

The apportionment or allocation of taxes for county purposes among the towns and cities of a county is one situation where equalization rates are important. Town and city assessors assess property for county as well as town and city tax purposes. Typically, substantial differences exist among these local governments in a county in the average percentage of full value at which properties are assessed. To apportion taxes for county purposes among towns

---

[2] Hollis A. Swett, "Real Estate Value and the Property Tax, Some Basic Concepts," paper presented at the Association of Towns Annual Meeting, New York, New York, February 1976.

and cities in proportion to total assessed values in each town and city would be manifestly unfair. Equalization rates, therefore, are used to make adjustment.

Let us illustrate by a greatly simplified example. Suppose a county needs $900 of property taxes to help meet expenses for the coming, year. There are only two towns (and no cities) in the county, each with its own assessor. In Town A there are only three properties, each assessed at its full value of $30,000, $20,000, and $10,000. Total assessed value in Town A is, therefore, $60,000. The equalization rate, or average percentage of full value, at which properties are assessed is, therefore, the same as assessed value, $60,000.

In Town B, there are also three properties, each identical in full value to those in Town A. The assessor, however, has assessed each one at $10,000, making a total assessed value of $30,000, or one-half the total in Town A. The equalization rate for Town B should, therefore, be 50 percent. The $30,000 divided by 50 percent yields a full value of $60,000.

Let us further suppose that the tax levy of $900 for county purposes were to be apportioned between the two towns in proportion to their assessed values of $60,000 and $30,000. Taxpayers in Town A would bear two-thirds of the levy, or $600, since assessed value in Town A is two-thirds of the county total of $90,000. Taxpayers in Town B would bear one-third of the levy, or $300. Taxpayers in Town A would be paying double the amount of county tax compared with those in Town B although the full value of taxable property is identical in the two towns. The assessor for Town A, in conscientiously appraising each property at full value, would have penalized the taxpayers of the town. In Town B, the assessor has not only assessed all but one property at less than full value, but has failed to assess the three properties at a reasonably uniform percentage of their full value.

The law, therefore, provides for equalizing or adjusting assessed values of towns and cities in allocating county taxes. The equalization rate is the major factor in this adjustment. Essentially, taxes for county purposes are apportioned in proportion to full value of taxable property in each town or city.

To return to the example above, the assessed value of $60,000 in Town A divided by the equalization rate of 100 percent yields a full value of $60,000. The $30,000 assessed value in Town B divided by the 50 percent equalization rate yields a full value of $60,000. If the $900 of county taxes are apportioned in proportion to full value, the taxpayers of each town bear one-half the levy, or $450. Each town shares equally in the levy because the total full valuation in each town is the same.

The equalization rates correct for differences in average levels of assessment between the two towns. Note, however, that they do not correct for inequitable assessments on individual properties within a town. In Town B, for example, the three properties are assessed at $10,000 each although their value is $30,000, $20,000, and $10,000, respectively. Each property owner would have to pay one-third of the $450 county tax apportioned to the town although the full value of the first property is three times that of the third. In Town A, on the other hand, the three properties identical in value to those in Town B, have been assessed at full value, totaling $60,000. The tax rate of $7.50 per $1,000 required to raise $450 for county purposes in Town A would result in taxes of $225 against the $30,000 property, $150 against the $20,000 property, and #$75 against the $10,000 property. The assessor of Town B can correct inequitable assessments among individual properties in that town. An equalization rate cannot do this.

The assessor of Town B could correct the inequities by raising all assessments to full value as in Town A, by assessing each property at the current equalization rate level of 50 percent of full value, or by assessing each property at some other uniform percentage of full value. Instead of assessing the three properties at $10,000 each, the assessor could value the $30,000 property at $15,000, the $20,000 property at $10,000, and the $10,000 property at $5,000. Total assessed value would remain at $30,000, the equalization rate at 50 percent, and full value at $60,000. A tax rate of $15 per $1,000 assessed value would then be required to raise $450 of county taxes. Then, as in Town A, there would be taxes of $225 against the $30,000 property (assessed at $15,000), $150 against the $20,000 property (assessed at $10,000), and $75 against the $10,000 property (assessed at $5,000).

Importance of Accurate Equalization Rates. Although equalization rates do not correct for inequitable assessments on individual properties within a town, they can, as illustrated, effectively adjust for variations among towns (and cities) in average levels of value at which properties are assessed. They can do this to the degree that they are accurate.

Grossly inaccurate rates may be worse than none at all. For example, if the equalization rates in the illustration above were fixed at 100 percent for both Towns A and B, assessed value would be the same as full value in each town, and Town A would be penalized for its full value assessments. In effect, there would be no equalization rates or equalization of the tax levy for county purposes. If the equalization rates of both towns were fixed at 50 percent, the effect would be the same. If the rate for Town A were made lower than for Town B, Town A would be better off if the process were abolished. In any of these cases, Town A's assessor would have strong incentive to cut assessments on properties, and both towns could embark upon competitive undervaluation with chaotic results.

Two kinds of authorities are required to establish equalization rates annually: the state and the county. The state fixes rates for towns, cities, and villages. The county governing board, or a county equalization commission in a few counties, fixes rates for each town and city in that county. Appeal procedures are provided by state law for local jurisdictions that believe the state or county rates are unfair.

The county rates are used in apportioning taxes for county purposes among the towns and cities in the county. A county may adopt the state rates, and many do.

The state rates serve a variety of purposes. One of them, for example, is in distributing certain forms of state aid, especially state aid to school districts. A major part of state aid for education is distributed according to formulas that include as one factor the full valuation of taxable property in a school district. Full valuation is obtained by dividing assessed valuation by the state equalization rate, as in the illustrations above. School districts with a low full value of taxable property per pupil generally receive more state aid per pupil than their opposites.

The belief sometimes gains currency that raising the levels of assessed values in a community will curtail state aid for schools. As the examples above illustrate, this is not true so long as the state equalization rates reflect levels of assessment with reasonable accuracy, and the state uses the rates to calculate state aid.

In the present system of property taxation in New York, reasonably accurate equalization rates are essential for equitable allocation of property taxes and state aid, and for other purposes. They also help to assure those assessors who conscientiously try to readjust assessed values of properties in their communities that their efforts will not be penalized through apportionment of taxes and state aid.

PROPERTY SUBJECT TO TAX

Only real estate or real property (as defined in the Real Property Tax Law) is subject to the property tax in New York State, contrary to practice in many other states where all or part of personal property is also supposed to be included. All real property in the state is taxable unless exempt by law or other provision.

Exemptions, however, are substantial. In some assessing jurisdictions, they comprise the lion's share of all real estate. The more the exemptions, of course, the less the taxable property that remains to bear tax levies.

Exempt property includes not only that of governments (federal, state, and local) with certain exceptions, but also a variety of kinds of real estate held by various kinds of private organizations and individuals for various purposes. For example, property of churches, colleges, hospitals and charitable organizations used exclusively for nonprofit purposes is exempt. Certain railroad real property is entitled to partial exemption, as are certain agricultural and forest lands and business investments in real estate improvement. Property of war veterans and certain near relatives is entitled to exemption of up to $5,000, if purchased wi6th funds obtained from pensions and other sources provided by the federal or New York governments. Persons over 65 years old with limited incomes may be eligible for partial exemption of their homes. These examples are by no means comprehensive.

Generally, the kinds of exemptions have been growing in scope and complexity over a long period. The intended effect of state (and local) legislation of exemptions is, of course, to aid worthy causes, organizations, or individuals. A side effect is gradual erosion of the tax base as the list of exempt properties lengthens.

FULL VALUE ASSESSMENT

In no New York assessing jurisdiction—town, city, village or county—are all properties assessed precisely at full value. In very few does even the average level of assessment approximate 100 percent of full value.

These deficiencies in the statutory standard of perfection have a variety of causes. One is that property appraisal is not a precise science. Another is the lag between changing real estate values and the capacity of the governmental assessment machinery to keep up with them. Still another over the sweep of the long history of the state has been the absence of substantial support among local and state officials and other citizens for assessments uniformly approximating full value, except for occasional upsurges of revivalistic fervor in some localities, and even more rarely in the state capitol.

The Governor's Advisory Panel of Consultants reported in 1976 on an analysis of a sample of residential properties drawn from the 1973 state equalization survey.[3] The average ratio of assessment to sales was calculated, and then the average deviation of the assessment-to-sales ratio of each property from the sample average was determined (the coefficient of variation). In only 68 of 991 towns and cities in the state (excluding New York City) was the average deviation within 20 percent of the average assessment-sales ratio for that municipality. The average deviation was over 60 percent in 91 cities and towns. Said the panel, "[In] all but a handful of assessing units in New York State, assessments of residential property are scattered with appalling randomness over a wide range of deviation from the simple mean."[4] This comment was inspired, not simply by the failure to assess residences at full value, but by the failure to assess with reasonable consistency at any ratio of full value.

The panel chose to study residences probably partly because there are many more of them than other kinds of property and they are easier to appraise with some consistency. Other information shows wide variation in assessment of other properties and in average assessments of different classes of property.

As for overall average levels of assessment within assessing units, the state equalization rates for assessment rolls completed in 1975, the latest available year, are revealing. In only 60 of the 991 towns and cities were the rates within 10 percent of the full value standard (100

---

[3] Governor Hugh L. Carey, *Educational Finance and the New York State Real Property Tax—The Inescapable Relationship*, May 1976, Education Study Unit, N.Y. State Division of the Budget, State Capitol, Albany, New York 12224, 32 pp.
[4] Ibid., p. 7.

percent).[5] The rates themselves reflect market values at the January 1, 1973 price level, indicating that the State Board of Equalization and Assessment, like the local assessing units, has problems keeping up with changing real estate values.

The extreme range in equalization rates among towns and cities was from 1.16 percent in the town of Highland, Sullivan County to 136.36 percent in the Town of Manlius, Onondaga County. Within some counties the range was similarly very great. Within Ulster County, for example, the rates were 131.86 and 3.55 percent, respectively, in the Towns of Denning and Hardenburgh. In Westchester County, the Town of Cortlandt had a rate of 17.18 percent, and North Salem, 105.94 percent. In New York City, which is a single assessing district, the range among its five counties was from 36.57 percent in Richmond to 70.29 percent in New York.

Equalization rates were below 30 percent in 616 of the 991 towns and cities, and below 50 percent in 778. They exceeded 100 percent in 43 municipalities. In recent years, the rates have tended rapidly downward as the rise in real estate prices has accelerated faster than the great majority of assessors have reappraised their assessment rolls. One indication of the trend is that the State Board of Equalization and Assessment decided to add two decimals to the equalization rates beginning with 1974 assessment rolls; some are so low (for instance, the Town of Highland cited above) that a change of one whole percentage point would raise full value by a very large proportion.

In this situation of "appalling randomness" of assessment of individual properties, and declining equalization rates in a rising real estate market, the New York Court of Appeals, the highest state court, decided that the New York Real Property Tax Law requires assessment at full (market) value. On June 5, 1975, the court ordered that the Town of Islip in Suffolk County assess all real property within the Town at full value by December 31, 1976 (a deadline that was later delayed).[6] Although the "Hellerstein" decision was directed only to the Town of Islip, it binds the lower courts to uphold a similar challenge in any other assessing district. As of April 1977, at least 36 "Hellerstein-type" actions had been filed in courts throughout the state, and more undoubtedly will follow.

One of the taxpayer suits was against the Nassau County Board of Assessors, which a lower state court ordered in May 1977 to complete new assessment rolls at full value by May 1, 1980. The chairman of the board was quoted as saying, "Our present rolls date back to 1938...Since then the value of residential property has climbed sharply while commercial property has not risen as much."[7] The 1975 equalization rate for the county was 17.12 percent.

These developments are stimulating widespread interest in bringing assessments to full value and maintaining them from year to year at that changing level. These are difficult goals not attained statewide over the nearly 200 years that the state law has required assessment at full value or its equivalent. They had not been attained in other states with comparable assessment standards although the high courts of several states have rendered similar decisions—among them New Jersey, 1975; Connecticut, 1957; and Massachusetts, 1961.

The potential benefits of full value assessments are substantial. First, taxes on similar properties in the same tax districts would be equalized. (The same result would of course follow from consistent assessment at some fraction of full value.) Second, taxpayers are more likely to have some knowledge of the accuracy of their properties' assessed values in comparison to their market values, as opposed to some (often unknown) average fractional assessment in the district. Finally, taxpayers are more likely to challenge an excessive assessment if it exceeds their estimate of true value; a fractional assessment at far less than full value is less likely to

---

[5] N.Y. State Board of Equalization and Assessment, *State Equalization Rates for 1975 Assessment Rolls for Cities, Towns and Villages*, October 1976, 23 pp.
[6] Pauline Hellerstein v. The Assessor of the Town of Islip.
[7] *New York Times*, May 24, 1977.

create taxpayer concern, even if it is excessive in relation to assessments of comparable properties.

Full value assessment (or for that matter, consistent assessment at a percentage of full value) would inevitably cause a shift of taxes among individual properties and among different classes of property. This is an inevitable outcome of equalizing assessments of properties having equal full or market value. The studies done for the governor's panel (cited above) by the State Board of Equalization and Assessment and the Education Unit of the State Division of the Budget indicate that the shifts in taxes within the residential property class from one property to another would total far more than the shift from other property classes to the residential category.[8] Among classes, however, estimated statewide totals indicate a probable net tax shift to residential, vacant land, and farm property classes from the commercial, apartment, industrial, and utility classes.

It is hazardous to generalize from these statewide totals to a specific local situation because there is so much variation among assessing units. For example, these analyses indicate that, on the average over the state, commercial properties are over-assessed compared with residential and farm properties, but in a specific town this average relationship may not hold and the reverse situation can even be true. The average relationship is still less likely to prevail in comparing individual properties in a town, because the variation in ratios of assessment to full value within a property class such as residences is extreme in many towns and cities.

Once a number of revaluation programs have been completed in many assessing units, it will be possible to determine whether particular classes of taxpayers are unduly burdened. If such a burden results, some sort of relief could be granted by the State Legislature. Among many alternatives is legislating that certain types of property be assessed at a specified percentage of full value. If fractional assessment is authorized, however, it will still be necessary to determine the full values upon which the fractions can be based in a consistent manner. Other alternatives, such as partial exemption of single family residences, are also likely to require determining full values as a yardstick for exemptions.

COMPUTER-ASSISTED ASSESSMENTS

In trying to make assessment rolls conform more nearly to the statutory standard of full value or some uniform percentage of full value in a thorough-going, professional and equitable way, the assessors have commonly reappraised or revalued all properties. Alternatively, local governments have contracted with appraisal firms to do the work with the resulting values subject to acceptance by their assessors. Counties have often contracted for revaluation for their constituent towns and cities in anticipation of greater countywide uniformity in assessment.

A major limitation of this procedure has been the difficulty of keeping the information and values up-to-date once they have been compiled. Massive amounts of data must be accumulated and analyzed on a continuing basis. This is usually much beyond the capacity of the assessing office with the resources commonly available. Revaluations have quickly become outdated because of rapidly changing real estate values and changes in existing properties, such as new construction, demolition, or other destruction of property.

Attempts to apply computer technology in recent years to these mass appraisal procedures offer promise of making it possible for the first time to keep assessment roll listings and valuations reasonably current. Computers may well make it practical for assessing districts to implement the Hellerstein decision by revaluing properties and keeping abreast of changing market values thereafter.

---

[8] Governor Hugh L. Carey, op. cit., p. 17.

The New York State Board of Equalization and Assessment over the past few years has been developing what it terms the Real Property Information System, which includes computer assistance for property valuation. The system has been implemented by assessors of several local governments beginning with the Town of Ramapo (Rockland County). It provides assessors with the means of processing and updating market value information for all properties on assessment rolls.

Basically, the computer-assisted assessment procedure involves tabulating and recording all recent property sales in a jurisdiction. When a single-family residence is subjected to value estimating, this process is carried out:

1. The computer selects the five properties from the sales file that most closely resemble the one being appraised.
2. The computer calculates a predicted value for the subject residence. These calculations are based on the procedures customarily used by appraisers in judging value.
3. Once the computer estimates are generated, each one is reviewed by a professional appraisal at the property. If errors are found, appropriate information is fed back into the computer.

Computer-assisted assessments are most accurate for single-family residences, primarily because accurate comparable sales data for them are more readily available than for other kinds of property. Approximately 70 percent of the properties in the State (not including New York City) are in the residential class.[9] More than half the remainder, or almost a fifth of the total, is in the "vacant lands" class. The next most numerous properties are in the "commercial" and "farm" classes.

There are nearly 1,000 town, city, and county assessing districts in the state with approximately 3.5 million parcels outside New York City to be assessed. At best, full-scale implementation of computerized assessments will be a lengthy process. Current budgetary and staff restrictions, and attrition of the State Board of Equalization and Assessment's experienced professional personnel, will make it even more protracted. Historically, the state and the public have shown only desultory interest in matching assessment performance with statutory standards and these cutbacks are consistent with that record.[10]

ASSESSORS

Assessing units in New York include almost all towns and cities, some villages, two counties, and the state itself. The State Board of Equalization and Assessment is responsible for assessing some properties, principally special franchises and railroad property in connection with fixing ceilings for partial exemptions. Special franchise property is generally property of public utilities located in public lands, for example, a power or telephone line in a highway right of way.

Two counties—Nassau and Tompkins—are assessing units.[11] Elsewhere in the state, the 918 towns and 59 cities are assessing units; and their assessment rolls are used for town and city, special district, county and school taxation. The village board of trustees can also elect to

---

[9] Governor Hugh L. Carey, op. cit., p. 23.

[10] See Postscript at end of this bulletin. Recent legislation may speed implementation of computer-assisted assessments.

[11] In Nassau, the two cities (Glen Cove and Long Beach) and the 65 villages may assess for city and village tax purposes, respectively.

have town assessments used for village taxation, rather than to have separate village assessments.

The "Assessment Improvement Law" of 1970, how officially Article 15-A of the Real Property Tax Law, made substantial changes in the assessment organization affecting local assessors, except in the villages and New York City.

One such change required the appointment of one assessor in each district meeting minimum qualification standards who was to undergo training determined by the State Board of Equalization and Assessment. This assessor is appointed by the local legislative body (or chief executive in some cases) for a six-year term, unless the position has an indefinite term in the competitive civil service. The appointee may be removed, but only for just cause. Exceptions to this appointive single assessor requirement were made for Nassau County and cities of 100,000 or more population (New York, Buffalo, Rochester, Yonkers, Syracuse, Albany). Another important exception is that over half the towns and a few smaller cities opted before the prescribed deadline in 1971 to retain their traditional practice of electing a single assessor, or, as in most towns, a three-person board (two elected at each biennial town election, one for a two-year and the other for a four-year term). The only qualification the law requires of a candidate for election as an assessor has been that he or she be a voter of the town. Municipalities that exercised the option of electing their assessors, nevertheless, must conform with the assessor training and other requirements of the Assessment Improvement Law. These municipalities may also opt to shift to appointing a single assessor, and some have since 1971. It should be said that a number of cities and towns had appointed professional assessors and assessment staffs long before this law was passed.

A second change required by Article 15-A for cities and towns is appointment of a board of assessment review composed of persons who are not assessors and a majority of whom are not officers or employees of the local government. The board hears taxpayer complaints on grievance day. Prior to the new law, the assessors of most local governments sat as a board of review. The intent of the change was to meet criticism of long standing that the assessors sat as judges of their own work, to hear and make decisions on taxpayer appeals from their own work.

The governing body of the local government must appoint from three to five review board members who have knowledge of property values in the locality. Membership could include, for example, individuals engaged in banking, insurance, real estate, professional appraising and similar occupations, and persons formerly assessors. Appointments are for five-year staggered terms.

TAXPAYER COMPLAINT AND APPEAL PROVISIONS

Assessors in each town and city not governed by special provisions are expected to assess all real property within their jurisdiction (except special franchises) according to its condition and ownership as of May 1.[12] The law requires completion of the tentative assessment roll on or before June 1. A copy must be left with the assessor or the town clerk for public inspection, and notices must be posted in the town and published in a newspaper. At least ten days before grievance day, the assessor must mail notices to those on whose property assessments have been increased.

---

[12] There are differences from the dates named in this section for the special "tax act" counties of Erie, Monroe, Nassau, Suffolk, and Westchester. Tompkins is such a county also, but the dates do not differ except for the city of Ithaca. For most villages, the date of taxable status is January 1; for tentative completion of the village assessment roll, February 1; and for village grievance day, the 3rd Tuesday in February.

Grievance day is held on the third Tuesday in June at the time and place specified in the public notices. Complaining taxpayers may file a statement under oath indicating why the assessment of their property is incorrect. The board of assessment review receives and hears complaints on grievance day, and may adjust up or down the assessments under question. The assessor must attend (in other words, sit with) the tentative assessment roll on at least three days of the public inspection period prior to grievance day. He or she must also attend the review board hearings, and has the right to respond to any complaint. Informal complaints may of course be made to assessors the year-round.

On or before August 1, the assessor completes the assessment roll. The assessor then must file a certified copy of the roll with the town or city clerk where it is open for public inspection. Notices to this effect must be published in a local newspaper, and, in towns, posted at the town clerk's office. The original roll is delivered to the clerk of the county legislative body, and town, special district, and county taxes are entered on it usually late in the fall. It is delivered to the tax collector with a warrant for collection, usually by the first of the year. The taxes must also be entered on the copy of the roll that remains in the town clerk's office as a public record.

If a complaining taxpayer fails to obtain the relief desired at the grievance day proceedings, he or she may carry an appeal to the courts. In presenting the case to a court, the taxpayer must establish the full market value of his or her property and the average level of assessment in the assessing unit. Court appeals, historically an expensive and time-consuming process used by few taxpayers, have been substantially simplified in the last several years by amendments to the law, and more recently by important court decisions. In *Ed Guth Realty v. Gingold*, a case from the City of Syracuse, the Court of Appeals ruled in 1974 that the state equalization rate can be used as the most significant evidence toward satisfying the burden of proof of the average level of assessment in the assessing unit. Shortly thereafter, the ruling was regarded as applicable in another local government in the case of *860 Executive Towers Inc. v. The Board of Assessors of the County of Nassau*. The court (Appellate Division) further concluded that, although the methods used by the State Board of Equalization and Assessment can be improved, they cannot be challenged in a proceeding to review an assessment.[13]

The taxpayer thus has to show in court only that the level of assessment on his or her property is higher than the average level of assessment indicated by the state equalization rate.[14] A customarily long and costly process for the taxpayer of appraising a sample of comparable properties in the jurisdiction is thereby apparently eliminated.

As a result of these decisions, it is said that thousands of similar cases are pending throughout the state.

SOME IMPLICATIONS FOR ASSESSING UNITS

The court decisions in the Guth and Hellerstein cases have helped to open a Pandora's box for assessors, the courts, local governments, state legislative and executive agencies, and perhaps many taxpayers.

Any taxpayer willing to go to the trouble and expense may ask a court to require a revaluation of the assessment rolls at full value in his or her town or city, relying on the Hellerstein case. Any taxpayers who feel that their properties are assessed at a substantially higher ratio than the equalization rate for their towns or cities, may apply to a court for a reduction in assessment, relying on the Guth case rulings.

---

[13] Association of Towns of the State of New York, *Assessors Topics*, October 1976, Albany, New York.
[14] The 1977 State Legislature amended the Real Property Tax Law to qualify in an uncertain way the impact of the Guth decision. See Postscript for further discussion of this change.

An assessing unit can, as many have, anticipate the prospect of a revaluation at full value, and prepare for it. Computer-assisted assessment is one possible line of action already discussed. In practical terms, however, this alternative is probably contingent upon the availability of competent and persistent state support. The prospects for it on the massive scale needed to work with large numbers of local governments and parcels of property are not encouraging in this period of retrenchment. However, one favorable development is 1977 legislation that provides state aid for part of the cost of local revaluation.

The assessing unit, because of the Guth case and for other reasons, also can examine carefully the data used by the State Board of Equalization and Assessment in fixing the equalization rate for that unit. When a Guth-type case arises, it is too late to question the rate in court. The state sampling, appraisals, and other steps and information in the rate-fixing process, can be challenged with solid evidence when found questionable, but this should be done as early in the procedure as possible, and at least by the time the State Board sends notice of the tentative equalization rate.

It is to the advantage of the state as well as local governments and taxpayers that its equalization rates be as accurate as practicable. To improve accuracy, local assessors and governments have customarily been encouraged to contribute information. Among other ways of eliciting information, the State Board has sought through field staff to check its sampling with local officials. The Board has also freely supplied local officials with the data behind its equalization rate, and has acted upon information supplied by them when it is pertinent, substantial, and objective.

In the current period of curtailment and retrenchment, the open relations between state and local governments desired for more accurate equalization rates are in jeopardy. From the local viewpoint, the State Board has reduced local contacts, supplied data less promptly and freely, and given notice of tentative equalization rates so late that studied response is impractical. Efforts toward improving equity in assessment, according to its statutory definition, can be crippled in such a situation. Equalization rates also can gradually deteriorate—as they in fact did earlier in the history of the state[15]—and the state becomes quite remote to a city or town assessor.

COUNTY AND STATE SERVICES FOR LOCAL ASSESSORS

Another major provision of the Assessment Improvement Law of 1970 is that counties and the State Board of Equalization and Assessment provide various forms of technical and professional aid to local assessing units.[16]

County Services. Each county except the two (Nassau and Tompkins) now acting as assessing units has been required to establish a real property tax service agency, and to appoint a director for a six-year term to head it. The law has required the director to meet minimum qualifications set by the State Board, and complete the training courses it prescribes, as with town and city assessors. Appraisers employed by the county agency must meet the same conditions.

In general, the purpose of the agency is to assist towns and cities with assessments and assessing work, and to do work for the county that has been associated with assessing and taxing real property. It must prepare tax maps, keep them up-to-date and provide copies to city,

---

[15] For example, grossly inaccurate rates led to creating in 1949 the present State Board of Equalization and Assessment.
[16] Real Property Tax Law, Article 15-A.

town, and village assessors and others. The initial maps must be completed and State Board approved applied for by October 1, 1979.

At the request of the chief executive or assessor of cities and towns in the county, the agency was to be ready by October 1, 1976, to perform advisory appraisals of "moderately complex properties" requiring engineering skills, or economic analyses of "substantial complexity." The State Board determines the specific types of property included in this provision. It must also review agency appraisals if the town or city assessor thinks them inaccurate or unreasonable and applies for review. The appraisals are not binding upon city or town assessors but must be considered by them.

The county agency must also advise assessors concerning assessment rolls, property record cards, appraisal cards, and other records. It must provide appraisal cards in the form prescribed by the State Board and cooperate in training programs of the Board. It must also provide useful information to the county authorities for fixing town and city equalization rates for county tax purposes, and perform other duties.

State Services. An important responsibility of the State Board not already described is that it was to be prepared by October 1, 1976, to do advisory appraisals of (1) privately owned forest lands in excess of 500 acres, (2) "highly complex properties" requiring highly specialized engineering skills or highly complex economic analyses, and (3) taxable public utility property. These appraisals must be done, as in the case of the county, at the request of the local government's chief executive or assessor.

THE GAP BETWEEN LAW AND PRACTICE

The gap between the legal requirement of full value assessment and local performance is great, and so is the gap between what the state is supposed to do and actually does.

With respect to local deficiencies, many factors contribute to the "appalling randomness" of assessment described by the Governor's Panel. Among them is the deviation of local practice from the idea embodied in the Assessment Improvement Law of 1970 that assessing personnel should be appointed by local governing boards rather than elected, that these individuals should have at least a minimum of prior professional training or experienced or both, and that they should have some assurance of at least a minimum job tenure consistent with conscientious work performance. Approximately half the towns and a few cities apparently continue to elect assessors and each biennial local election results in high turnover, with sometimes cavalier voter disregard for consistent and persistent assessment. Building expertise in functions such as computer-assisted assessments in a locality under these circumstances is probably impossible.

Local boards of assessment review ideally have a quasi-judicial role of correcting injustice, when they hear formal complaints, by referring to the Guth case and related high court decisions and laws. Some local boards can make a shambles of uniform assessment by granting practically any request for reduced valuation. Others can tolerate poor assessment by refusing relief, however, judicially justified it may be.

With respect to counties, considerable variation exists in their capacity to complete and maintain tax maps, perform advisory appraisals, and assist town and city assessing units in other ways prescribed by the Assessment Improvement Law of 1970.

The gap between State Board performance and the requirements of the Real Property Tax Law is substantial. The Board is not providing systematic training for local assessing and appraisal personnel. It has postponed advisory appraisals beyond the legal deadline of October 1, 1976. It lacks the capacity to lend technical assistance and support for widespread local implementation of computer-assisted assessments and other aspects of its Real Property

Information System. It is making more difficult local opportunity for close scrutiny of equalization rates.

Curtailment and retrenchment of State Board activities is inconsistent with the expansion of state responsibilities required by law and recent major judicial decisions. Such reduction is at least partly the result of the more general and severe fiscal pressures upon the state.

The state and local situations do not, and should not, encourage taxpayer belief in early achievement of statewide equity of property assessment according to the statutory definition of equity. It is possible, however, to improve local performance within the present framework in those localities where the will exists and resources are committed to achieve improvement.

CONCLUSION

Inequities in assessing properties are common in New York except in those communities taking vigorous steps to bring assessed value into line with current real estate market values. Reducing inequities by a thorough revaluation or reassessment does not necessarily result in increased taxes for individuals. It will result in a larger share of taxes for those whose properties have been under-assessed compared with their neighbors. A smaller share will be borne by property owners over-assessed theretofore compared with their neighbors.

GLOSSARY OF REAL ESTATE TERMS

CONTENTS

	Page
Abstract of Title................Appraisal by Summation	1
Appurtenance.......................Cancellation Clause	2
Caveat Emptor...............................Conveyance	3
County Clerk's Certificate.... Documentary Evidence	4
Duress....................................Exclusive Agency	5
Exclusive Right to Sell......................Ground Rent	6
Habendum Clause................................ Landlord	7
Lease...Mortgagee	8
Mortgagor...Party Wall	9
Percentage Lease...................................Release	10
Release Clause....................Subordination Clause	11
Subscribing Witness..............................Valuation	12
Vendee's Lien.... ....Zoning Ordinance	13

GLOSSARY OF REAL ESTATE TERMS
A

Abstract of Title—A summary of all of the recorded instruments and proceedings which affect the title to property, arranged in chronological order.

Accretion—The addition to land through processes of nature, as by streams or wind.

Accrued Interest—Accrue: to grow; to be added to. Accrued interest is interest that has been earned but not due and payable.

Acknowledgment—A formal declaration before a duly authorized officer by a person who has executed an instrument that such execution is the person's act and deed.

Acquisition—An act or process by which a person procures property.

Acre—A measure of land equaling 160 square rods or 4,840 square yards or 43,560 feet.

Adjacent—Lying near to but not necessarily in actual contact with.

Adjoining—Contiguous; attaching, in actual contact with.

Administrator—A person appointed by court to administer the estate of a deceased person who left no will; i.e., who died intestate.

Ad Valorem—According to valuation.

Adverse Possession—A means of acquiring title where an occupant has been in actual, open, notorious, exclusive, and continuous occupancy of property under a claim of right for the required statutory period.

Affidavit—A statement or declaration reduced to writing, and sworn to or affirmed before some officer who is authorized to administer an oath or affirmation.

Affirm—To confirm, to ratify, to verify.

Agency—That relationship between principal and agent which arises out of a contract either expressed or implied, written or oral, wherein an agent is employed by a person to do certain acts on the person's behalf in dealing with a third party.

Agent—One who undertakes to transact some business or to manage some affair for another by authority of the latter.

Agreement of Sale—A written agreement between seller and purchaser in which the purchaser agrees to buy certain real estate and the seller agrees to sell upon terms and conditions set forth therein.

Alienation—A transferring of property to another; the transfer of property and possession of lands, or other things, from one person to another

Amortization—A gradual paying off of a debt by periodical installments.

Apportionments—Adjustment of the income, expenses or carrying charges of real estate usually computed to the date of closing of title so that the seller pays all expenses to that date. The buyer assumes all expenses commencing the date the deed is conveyed to the buyer.

Appraisal—An estimate of a property's valuation by an appraiser who is usually presumed to be expert in this work.

Appraisal by Capitalization—An estimate of value by capitalization of productivity and income.

Appraisal by Comparison—Comparability with the sale prices of other similar properties.

Appraisal by Summation—Adding together all parts of a property separately appraised to form a whole: e.g., value of the land considered as vacant added to the cost of reproduction of the building, less depreciation.

Appurtenance—Something which is outside the property itself but belongs to the land and adds to its greater enjoyment such as a right of way or a barn or a dwelling.

Assessed Valuation—A valuation placed upon property by a public officer or a board, as a basis for taxation.

Assessment—A charge against real estate made by a unit of government to cover a proportionate cost of an improvement such as a street or sewer.

Assessor—An official who has the responsibility of determining assessed values.

Assignee—The person to whom an agreement or contract is assigned.

Assignment—The method or manner by which a right, a specialty, or contract is transferred from one person to another.

Assignor—A party who assigns or transfers an agreement or contract to another.

Assumption of Mortgage—The taking of title to property by a grantee, wherein the grantee assumes liability for payment of an existing note or bond secured by a mortgage against a property and becomes personally liable for the payment of such mortgage debt.

Attest—To witness to; to witness by observation and signature.

Avulsion—The removal of land from one owner to another, when a stream suddenly changes its channel.

B

Beneficiary—The person who receives or is to receive the benefits resulting from certain acts.

Bequeath—To give or hand down by will; to leave by will.

Bequest—That which is given by the terms of a will.

Bill of Sale—A written instrument given to pass title of personal property from vendor to vendee.

Binder—An agreement to cover the down payment for the purchase of real estate as evidence of good faith on the part of the purchaser.

Blanket Mortgage—A single mortgage which covers more than one piece of real estate.

Bona Fide—In good faith, without fraud.

Bond—The evidence of a personal debt which is secured by a mortgage or other lien on real estate.

Building Codes—Regulations established by local governments stating fully the structural requirements for building.

Building Line—A line fixed at a certain distance from the front and/or sides of a lot, beyond which no building can project.

Building Loan Agreement—An agreement whereby the lender advances money to an owner with provisional payments at certain stages of construction.

C

Cancellation Clause—A provision in a lease which confers upon one or more or all of the parties to the lease the right to terminate the party's or parties' obligations thereunder upon the occurrence of the condition or contingency set forth in the said clause.

Caveat Emptor—Let the buyer beware. The buyer must examine the goods or property and buy at the buyer's own risk.

Cease and Desist Order—An order executed by the Secretary of State directing broker recipients to cease and desist from all solicitation of homeowners whose names and addresses appear on the list(s) forwarded with such order. The order acknowledges petition filings by homeowners listed evidencing their premises are not for sale, thereby revoking the implied invitation to solicit. The issuance of a Cease and Desist Order does not prevent an owner from selling or listing his premises for sale. It prohibits soliciting by licensees served with such order and subjects violators to penalties of suspension or revocation of their licenses as provided in section 441-c of the Real Property Law.

Cease and Desist Petition—A statement filed by a homeowner showing address of premises owned which notifies the Department of State that such premises are not for sale and does not wish to be solicited. In so doing, petitioner revokes the implied invitation to be solicited, by any means with respect thereto, by licensed real estate brokers and salespersons.

Certiorari—A proceeding to review in a competent court the action of an inferior tribunal board or officer exercising judicial functions.

Chain of Title—A history of conveyances and encumbrances affecting a title from the time the original patent was granted, or as far back as records are available.

Chattel—Personal property, such as household goods or fixtures.

Chattel Mortgage—A mortgage on personal property.

Client—The one by whom a broker is employed and by whom the broker will be compensated on completion of the purpose of the agency.

Closing Date—The date upon which the buyer takes over the property; usually between 30 and 60 days after the signing of the contract. Cloud on the Title An outstanding claim or encumbrance which, if valid, would affect or impair the owner's title.

Collateral—Additional security pledged for the payment of an obligation.

Color of Title—That which appears to be good title, but which is not title in fact.

Commission—A sum due a real estate broker for services in that capacity.

Commitment—A pledge or a promise or affirmation agreement.

Condemnation—Taking private property for public use, with fair compensation to the owner; exercising the right of eminent domain.

Conditional Sales Contract—A contract for the sale of property stating that delivery is to be made to the buyer, title to remain vested in the seller until the conditions of the contract have been fulfilled.

Consideration—Anything of value given to induce entering into a contract; it may be money, personal services, or even love and affection.

Constructive Notice—Information or knowledge of a fact imputed by law to a person because the person could have discovered the fact by proper diligence and inquiry; (public records).

Contract—An agreement between competent parties to do or not to do certain things for a legal consideration, whereby each party acquires a right to what the other possesses.

Conversion—Change from one character or use to another.

Conveyance—The transfer of the title of land from one to another. The means or medium by which title of real estate is transferred.

County Clerk's Certificate—When an acknowledgment is taken by an officer not authorized in the state or county where the document is to be recorded, the instrument which must be attached to the acknowledgment is called a county clerk's certificate. It is given by the clerk of the county where the officer obtained his/her authority and certifies to the officer's signature and powers.

Covenants—Agreements written into deeds and other instruments promising performance or nonperformance of certain acts, or stipulating certain uses or nonuse's of the property.

D

Damages—The indemnity recoverable by a person who has sustained an injury, either to his/her person, property or relative rights, through the act or default of another.

Decedent—One who is dead.

Decree Order issued by one in authority; an edict or law; a judicial decision.

Dedication—A grant and appropriation of land by its owner for some public use, accepted for such use, by an authorized public official on behalf of the public.

Deed—An instrument in writing duly executed and delivered, that conveys title to real property.

Deed Restriction—An imposed restriction in a deed for the purpose of limiting the use of the land such as: A restriction against the sale of liquor thereon. A restriction As to the size, type, value or placement of improvements that may be erected thereon.

Default—Failure to fulfill a duty or promise, or to discharge an obligation; omission or failure to perform any acts.

Defendant—The party sued or called to answer in any suit, civil or criminal, at law or in equity.

Deficiency Judgment—A judgment given when the security for a loan does not entirely satisfy the debt upon its default.

Delivery—The transfer of the possession of a thing from one person to another.

Demising Clause—A clause found in a lease whereby the landlord (lessor) leases and the tenant (lessee) takes the property.

Depreciation—Loss of value in real property brought about by age, physical deterioration, or functional or economic obsolescence.

Descent—When an owner of real estate dies intestate, the owner's property descends, by operation of law, to the owner's distributees.

Devise—A gift of real estate by will or last testament.

Devisee—One who receives a bequest of real estate made by will.

Devisor—One who bequeaths real estate by will.

Directional Growth—The location or direction toward which the residential sections of a city are destined or determined to grow.

Dispossess Proceedings—Summary process by a landlord to oust a tenant and regain possession of the premises for nonpayment of rent or other breach of conditions of the lease or occupancy.

Distributee—Person receiving or entitled to receive land as representative of the former owner.

Documentary Evidence—Evidence in the form of written or printed papers.

Duress—Unlawful constraint exercised upon a person whereby the person is forced to do some act against his will.

Earnest Money—Down payment made by a purchaser of real estate as evidence of good faith.

Easement—A right that may be exercised by the public or individuals on, over or through the lands of others.

Ejectment—A form of action to regain possession of real property, with damages for the unlawful retention; used when there is no relationship of landlord and tenant.

Eminent Domain—A right of the government to acquire property for necessary public use by condemnation; the owner must be fairly compensated.

Encroachment—A building, part of a building, or obstruction which intrudes upon or invades a highway or sidewalk or trespasses upon the property of another.

Encumbrance—Any right to or interest in land that diminishes its value. (Also Incumbrance)

Endorsement—An act of signing one's name on the back of a check or note, with or without further qualifications.

Equity—The interest or value which the owner has in real estate over and above the liens against it.

Equity of Redemption—A right of the owner to reclaim property before it is sold through foreclosure proceedings, by the payment of the debt, interest and costs.

Erosion—The wearing away of land through processes of nature, as by streams and winds.

Escheat—The reversion to the state of property in event the owner thereof dies, without leaving a will and has no distributees to whom the property may pass by lawful descent.

Escrow—A written agreement between two or more parties providing that certain instruments or property be placed with a third party to be delivered to a designated person upon the fulfillment or performance of some act or condition.

Estate—The degree, quantity, nature and extent of interest which a person has in real property.

Estate for Life—An estate or interest held during the terms of some certain person's life.

Estate in Reversion—The residue of an estate left for the grantor, to commence in possession after the termination of some particular estate granted by the grantor.

Estate at Will—The occupation of lands and tenements by a tenant for an indefinite period, terminable by one or both parties at will.

Estoppel Certificate—An instrument executed by the mortgagor setting forth the present status and the balance due on the mortgage as of the date of the execution of the certificate. A legal proceeding by a lessor landlord to recover possession of real property.

Eviction, Actual—Where one is, either by force or by process of law, actually put out of possession.

Eviction, Constructive—Any disturbance of the tenant's possessions by the landlord whereby the premises are rendered unfit or unsuitable for the purpose for which they were leased.

Eviction, Partial—Where the possessor of the premises is deprived of a portion thereof.

Exclusive Agency—An agreement of employment of a broker to the exclusion of all other brokers; if sale is made by any other broker during term of employment, broker holding exclusive agency is entitled to commissions in addition to the commissions payable to the broker who effected the transaction.

Exclusive Right to Sell—An agreement of employment by a broker under which the exclusive right to sell for a specified period is granted to the broker; if a sale during the term of the agreement is made by the owner or by any other broker, the broker holding such exclusive right to sell is nevertheless entitled to compensation.

Executor—A male person or a corporate entity or any other type of organization named or designated in a will to carry out its provisions as to the disposition of the estate of a deceased person.

Executrix—A woman appointed to perform the duties similar to those of an executor.

Extension Agreement—An agreement which extends the life of the mortgage to a later date.

F

Fee; Fee Simple; Fee Absolute—Absolute ownership of real property; a person has this type of estate where the person is entitled to the entire property with unconditional power of disposition during the person's life and descending to the person's distributees and legal representatives upon the person's death intestate.

Fiduciary—A person who on behalf of or for the benefit of another transacts business or handles money on property not the person's own; such relationship implies great confidence and trust.

Fixtures—Personal property so attached to the land or improvements as to become part of the real property.

Foreclosure—A procedure whereby property pledged as security for a debt is sold to pay the debt in the event of default in payments or terms.

Forfeiture—Loss of money or anything of value, by way of penalty due to failure to perform.

Freehold—An interest in real estate, not less than an estate for life. (Use of this term discontinued Sept. 1, 1967.)

Front Foot—A standard measurement, one foot wide, of the width of land, applied at the frontage on its street line. Each front foot extends the depth of the lot.

G

Grace Period—Additional time allowed to perform an act or make a payment before a default occurs.

Graduated Leases—A lease which provides for a graduated change at stated intervals in the amount of the rent to be paid; used largely in long term leases.

Grant—A technical term used in deeds of conveyance of lands to indicate a transfer. Grantee The party to whom the title to real property is conveyed.

Grantor—The person who conveys real estate by deed; the seller.

Gross Income—Total income from property before any expenses are deducted.

Gross Lease—A lease of property whereby the lessor is to meet all property charges regularly incurred through ownership.

Ground Rent—Earnings of improved property credited to earning of the ground itself after allowance made for earnings of improvements.

H

Habendum Clause—The "To Have and To Hold" clause which defines or limits the quantity of the estate granted in the premises of the deed.

Hereditaments—The largest classification of property; including lands, tenements and incorporeal property, such as rights of way.

Holdover Tenant—A tenant who remains in possession of leased property after the expiration of the lease term.

Hypothecate—To give a thing as security without the necessity of giving up possession of it.

I

In Rem—A proceeding against the realty directly; as distinguished from a proceeding against a person. (Used in taking land for nonpayment of taxes, etc.)

Incompetent—A person who is unable to manage his/her own affairs by reason of insanity, inbecility or feeble-mindedness.

Incumbrance—Any right to or interest in land that diminishes its value. (Also Encumbrance)

Injunction—A writ or order issued under the seal of a court to restrain one or more parties to a suit or proceeding from doing an act which is deemed to be inequitable or unjust in regard to the rights of some other party or parties in the suit or proceeding.

Installments—Parts of the same debt, payable at successive periods as agreed; payments made to reduce a mortgage.

Instrument—A written legal document; created to effect the rights of the parties. Interest

Rate—The percentage of a sum of money charged for its use.

Intestate—A person who dies having made no will, or leaves one which is defective in form, in which case the person's estate descends to the person's distributees.

Involuntary Lien—A lien imposed against property without consent of the owner, i.e., taxes, special assessments.

Irrevocable—Incapable of being recalled or revoked; unchangeable; unalterable.

J

Jeopardy—Peril, danger.

Joint Tenancy—Ownership of realty by two or more persons, each of whom has an undivided interest with the "right of survivorship."

Judgment—Decree of a court declaring that one individual is indebted to another, and fixing the amount of such indebtedness.

Junior Mortgage—A mortgage second in lien to a previous mortgage.

L

Laches—Delay or negligence in asserting one's legal rights.

Land, Tenements and Hereditaments—A phrase used in the early English Law, to express all sorts of property of the immovable class.

Landlord—One who rents property to another.

Lease—A contract whereby, for a consideration, usually termed rent, one who is entitled to the possession of real property transfers such rights to another for life, for a term of years, or at will. Leasehold The interest or estate which a lessee of real estate has therein by virtue of the lessee's lease.

Lessee—A person to whom property is rented under a lease.

Lessor—One who rents property to another under a lease.

Lien—A legal right or claim upon a specific property which attaches to the property until a debt is satisfied.

Lien (Mechanic's)—A notice filed with the County Clerk stating that payment has not been made for an improvement to real property. Life Estate The conveyance of title to property for the duration of the life of the grantee.

Life Tenant—The holder of a life estate.

Lis Pendens—A legal document, filed in the office of the county clerk giving notice that an action or proceeding is pending in the courts affecting the title to the property.

Listing—An employment contract between principal and agent, authorizing the agent to perform services for the principal involving the latter's property.

Litigation—The act of carrying on a lawsuit.

M

Mandatory—Requiring strict conformity or obedience.

Market Value—The highest price which a buyer, willing but not compelled to buy, would pay, and the lowest a seller, willing but not compelled to sell, would accept.

Marketable Title—A title which a court of equity considers to be so free from defect that it will enforce its acceptance by a purchaser.

Mechanic's Lien—A lien given by law upon a building or other improvement upon land, and upon the land itself, to secure the price of labor done upon, and materials furnished for, the improvement.

Meeting of the Minds—Whenever all parties to a contract agree to the exact terms thereof.

Metes and Bounds—A term used in describing the boundary lines of land, setting forth all the boundary lines together with their terminal points and angles.

Minor—A person under an age specified by law; under 18 years of age.

Monument—A fixed object and point established by surveyors to establish land locations.

Moratorium—An emergency act by a legislative body to suspend the legal enforcement of contractual obligations.

Mortgage—An instrument in writing, duly executed and delivered, that creates a lien upon real estate as security for the payment of a specified debt, which is usually in the form of a bond.

Mortgage Commitment—A formal indication, by a lending institution that it will grant a mortgage loan on property, in a certain specified amount and on certain specified terms. Mortgage Reduction Certificate An instrument executed by the mortgagee, setting forth the present status and the balance due on the mortgage as of the date of the execution of the instrument.

Mortgagee—The party who lends money and takes a mortgage to secure the payment thereof.

Mortgagor—A person who borrows money and gives a mortgage on the person's property as security for the payment of the debt.

Multiple Listing—An arrangement among Real Estate Board of Exchange Members, whereby each broker presents the broker's listings to the attention of the other members so that if a sale results, the commission is divided between the broker bringing the listing and the broker making the sale.

N

Net Listing—A price below which an owner will not sell the property, and at which price a broker will not receive a commission; the broker receives the excess over and above the net listing as the broker's commission.

Notary Public—A public officer who is authorized to take acknowledgments to certain classes of documents, such as deeds, contracts, mortgages, and before whom affidavits may be sworn.

O

Obligee—The person in whose favor an obligation is entered into.

Obligor—The person who binds himself/herself to another; one who has engaged to perform some obligation; one who makes a bond.

Obsolescence—Loss in value due to reduced desirability and usefulness of a structure because its design and construction become obsolete; loss because of becoming old-fashioned, and not in keeping with modern means, with consequent loss of income.

Open End Mortgage—A mortgage under which the mortgagor may secure additional funds from the mortgagee, usually up to but not exceeding the original amount of the existing amortizing mortgage.

Open Listing—A listing given to any number of brokers without liability to compensate any except the one who first secures a buyer ready, willing and able to meet the terms of the listing, or secures the acceptance by the seller of a satisfactory offer; the sale of the property automatically terminates the listing.

Open Mortgage—A mortgage that has matured or is overdue and, therefore, is "open" to foreclosure at any time.

Option—A right given for a consideration to purchase or lease a property upon specified terms within a specified time; if the right is not exercised the option holder is not subject to liability for damages; if exercised, the grantor of option must perform.

P

Partition—The division which is made of real property between those who own it in undivided shares.

Party Wall—A party wall is a wall built along the line separating two properties, partly on each, which wall either owner, the owner's heirs and assigns has the right to use; such right constituting an easement over so much of the adjoining owner's land as is covered by the wall.

Percentage Lease—A lease of property in which the rental is based upon the percentage of the volume of sales made upon the leased premises, usually provides for minimum rental.
Personal Property—Any property which is not real property.

Plat Book—A public record containing maps of land showing the division of such land into streets, blocks and lots and indicating the measurements of the individual parcels.

Plottage—Increment in unity value of a plot of land created by assembling smaller ownerships into one ownership.

Police Power—The right of any political body to enact laws and enforce them, for the order, safety, health, morals and general welfare of the public.

Power of Attorney—A written instrument duly signed and executed by an owner of property, which authorizes an agent to act on behalf of the owner to the extent indicated in the instrument.

Premises—Lands and tenements; an estate; the subject matter of a conveyance.

Prepayment Clause—A clause in a mortgage which gives a mortgagor the privilege of paying the mortgage indebtedness before it becomes due.

Principal—The employer of an agent or broker; the broker's or agent's client.

Probate—To establish the will of a deceased person.

Purchase Money Mortgage—A mortgage given by a grantee in part payment of the purchase price of real estate.

Q

Quiet Enjoyment—The right of an owner or a person legally in possession to the use of property without interference of possession.

Quiet Title Suit—A suit in court to remove a defect, cloud or suspicion regarding legal rights of an owner to a certain parcel of real property.

Quitclaim Deed—A deed which conveys simply the grantor's rights or interest in real estate, without any agreement or covenant as to the nature or extent of that interest, or any other covenants; usually used to remove a cloud from the title.

R

Real Estate Board—An organization whose members consist primarily of real estate brokers and salespersons.

Real Property—Land, and generally whatever is erected upon or affixed thereto.

Realtor—A coined word which may only be used by an active member of a local real estate board, affiliated with the National Association of Real Estate Boards.

Recording—The act of writing or entering in a book of public record instruments affecting the title to real property.

Redemption—The right of a mortgagor to redeem the property by paying a debt after the expiration date and before sale at foreclosure; the right of an owner to reclaim the owner's property after the sale for taxes.

Release—The act or writing by which some claim or interest is surrendered to another.

Release Clause—A clause found in a blanket mortgage which gives the owner of the property the privilege of paying off a portion of the mortgage indebtedness, and thus freeing a portion of the property from the mortgage.

Rem—(See In Rem)

Remainder—An estate which takes effect after the termination of a prior estate such as a life estate.

Remainderman—The person who is to receive the property after the death of a life tenant.

Rent—The compensation paid for the use of real estate.

Reproduction Cost—Normal cost of exact duplication of a property as of a certain date.

Restriction—A limitation placed upon the use of property contained in the deed or other written instrument in the chain of title. Reversionary Interest The interest which a person has in lands or other property upon the termination of the preceding estate.

Revocation—An act of recalling a power of authority conferred, as the revocation of a power of attorney, a license, an agency, etc.

Right of Survivorship—Right of the surviving joint owner to succeed to the interests of the deceased joint owner, distinguishing feature of a joint tenancy or tenancy by the entirety.

Right of Way—The right to pass over another's land more or less frequently according to the nature of the easement.

Riparian Owner—One who owns land bounding upon a river or watercourse.

Riparian Rights—The right of a landowner to water on, under or adjacent to his land.

S

Sales Contract—A contract by which the buyer and seller agree to terms of sale.

Satisfaction Piece—An instrument for recording and acknowledging payment of an indebtedness secured by a mortgage.

Seizin—The possession of land by one who claims to own at least an estate for life therein.

Set Back—The distance from the curb or other established line, within which no buildings may be erected.

Severalty—The ownership of real property by an individual, as an individual.

Special Assessment—An assessment made against a property to pay for a public improvement by which the assessed property is supposed to be especially benefited.

Specific Performance—A remedy in a court of equity compelling a defendant to carry out the terms of an agreement or contract.

Statute—A law established by an act of the Legislature.

Statute of Frauds—State law which provides that certain contracts must be in writing in order to be enforceable at law.

Stipulations—The terms within a written contract.

Straight Line Depreciation—A definite sum set aside annually from income to pay costs of replacing improvements, without reference to the interest it earns.

Subdivision—A tract of land divided into lots or plots suitable for home building purposes.

Subletting—A leasing by a tenant to another, who holds under the tenant.

Subordination Clause—A clause which permits the placing of a mortgage at a later date which takes priority over an existing mortgage.

Subscribing Witness—One who writes his/her name as witness to the execution of an instrument.

Surety—One who guarantees the performance of another; guarantor.

Surrender—The cancellation of a lease by mutual consent of the lessor and the lessee.

Surrogate's Court (Probate Court)—A court having jurisdiction over the proof of wills, the settling of estates and of citations.

Survey—The process by which a parcel of land is measured and its area ascertained; also the blueprint showing the measurements, boundaries and area.

T

Tax Sale—Sale of property after a period of nonpayment of taxes.

Tenancy in Common—An ownership of realty by two or more persons, each of whom has an undivided interest, without the "right of survivorship."

Tenancy by the Entirety—An estate which exists only between husband and wife with equal right of possession and enjoyment during their joint lives and with the "right of survivorship."

Tenancy at Will—A license to use or occupy lands and tenements at the will of the owner.

Tenant—One who is given possession of real estate for a fixed period or at will.

Tenant at Sufferance—One who comes into possession of lands by lawful title and keeps it afterwards without any title at all.

Testate—Where a person dies leaving a valid will.

Title—Evidence that owner of land is in lawful possession thereof; evidence of ownership.

Title Insurance—A policy of insurance which indemnifies the holder for any loss sustained by reason of defects in the title.

Title Search—An examination of the public records to determine the ownership and encumbrances affecting real property.

Torrens Title—System of title records provided by state law: it is a system for the registration of land titles whereby the state of the title, showing ownership and encumbrances, can be readily ascertained from an inspection of the "register of titles" without the necessity of a search of the public records.

Tort—A wrongful act, wrong, injury; violation of a legal right.

Transfer Tax—A tax charged under certain conditions on the property belonging to an estate.

U

Unearned Increment—An increase in value of real estate due to no effort on the part of the owner; often due to increase in population.

Urban Property—City property; closely settled property.

Usury—On a loan, claiming a rate of interest greater than that permitted by law.

V

Valid—Having force, or binding force; legally sufficient and authorized by law.

Valuation—Estimated worth or price. The act of valuing by appraisal.

Vendee's Lien—A lien against property under contract of sale to secure deposit paid by a purchaser.

Verification—Sworn statements before a duly qualified officer to the correctness of the contents of an instrument.

Violations—Act, deed or conditions contrary to law or permissible use of real property.

Void—To have no force or effect; that which is unenforceable.

Voidable—That which is capable of being adjudged void, but is not void unless action is taken to make it so.

W

Waiver—The renunciation, abandonment or surrender of some claim, right or privilege.

Warranty Deed—A conveyance of land in which the grantor warrants the title to the grantee.

Will—The disposition of one's property to take effect after death.

Without Recourse—Words used in endorsing a note or bill to denote that the future holder is not to look to the endorser in case of nonpayment.

Z

Zone—An area set off by the proper authorities for specific use; subject to certain restrictions or restraints.

Zoning Ordinance—Act of city or county or other authorities specifying type and use to which property may be put in specific areas.

Made in the USA
Middletown, DE
02 December 2020